Economics

SCOTLAND 2070
Healthy | Wealthy | Wise

Pikettys's *Capital in the Twenty-First Century*. Edward Fullbrook and Jamie Moran, eds.

Volume 1
The Economics Curriculum. Maria Alejandra Madi and Jack Reardon, eds

Volume 2:
Finance as Warfare. Michael Hudson

Volume 3:
Developing an Economics for the Post-crisis World. Steve Keen

Volume 4:
On the Use and Misuse of Theories and Models in Mainstream Economics. Lars Pålsson Syll

Volume 5:
Green Capitalism. The God that Failed. Richard Smith

Volume 6:
40 Critical Pointers for Students of Economics. Stuart Birks

Volume 7:
The European Crisis. Victor Beker and Beniamino Moro, eds.

Volume 8:
A Philosophical Framework for Rethinking Theoretical Economics and Philosophy of Economics. Gustavo Marqués

Volume 9:
Narrative Fixation in Economics. Edward Fullbrook

Volume 10:
Ideas Towards a New International Financial Architecture. Oscar Ugarteche, Alicia Payana and Maria Alejandra Madi, eds

Volume 11:
Trumponomics. Causes and Consequences. Edward Fullbrook and Jamie Morgan, eds.

Volume 12:
Capital and Justice. Gerson P. Lima and Maria Alejandra Madi, eds

Volume 13
SCOTLAND 2070. Healthy | Wealthy | Wise. Ian Godden, Hillary Sillitto and Dorothy Godden

SCOTLAND 2070
Healthy | Wealthy | Wise
An Ambitious Vision for Scotland's Future

Without the Politics

Ian Godden

Hillary Sillitto

Dorothy Godden

ISBN 978-1-84890-348-7

Published by College Publications (London)

http://www.collegepublications.co.uk

Cover design by Laraine Welch

Dedication

to our children and grandchildren,

and to all those who are committed to

building and stewarding a thriving Scotland —

healthier, wealthier, and wiser than now —

and to those who live in it.

Contents

Foreword

This is an impressive and scholarly book. It sets a demanding vision for both the people of Scotland and their chosen leaders. The vicissitudes of climate change will pose a plethora of risks to the well-being of Scots and the nation's economy, but could also advance some very significant opportunities to enhance and improve its health and prosperity.

In rising to these challenges, the inhabitants of Scotland will need to put the narrowness of traditional 20th and 21st century Scottish politics behind them and embrace the "can-do" attitudes that so characterised Scotland at the time of the Scottish Enlightenment and in the succeeding century, when Scotland became a "thought leader" in Europe and a world leader in shipbuilding and industrial production.

This book does well to avoid much of the politics and class warfare of the last 100 years, with a firm focus on the possible levers of opportunity. Scottish scientists, engineers, administrators, academics and entrepreneurs have set the pace in the past. In rising to these challenges and in exploring and developing some of the concepts and ideas contained in this book, over the next 50 years, there is an opportunity for all Scots to work together to enrich the nation, economically, physically, morally and spiritually, following the path so determinedly blazed in the period 1750-1900, by their forefathers.

The book has three key messages. First, Scotland can succeed in the new world if we act decisively and ambitiously to take advantage of new opportunities that we can see emerging. Second, these opportunities are there whatever our political choices. And third, success requires a 50-year view.

Hew Balfour

East Lothian, October 2020

Authors' Preface

"So, this book you're writing about Scotland's future, is it a pro-independence rant?" a friend asked us.

"The answer is no, absolutely not. We're not pro-independence, nor pro-union, nor pro-federalism. We're just pro Scotland. We want a good future for Scotland and all of its people. We want a country our grandchildren would want to live in, one that young Scots roaming the world will come back to settle in because of the opportunities it offers them."

But can Scotland do well in the new world that is emerging after the great disruption caused by Covid-19?

We have a vision for an economically, socially and environmentally successful Scotland. It's ambitious, yet feasible; and, in the spirit of "never waste a good crisis," it's easier to achieve after Covid-19 than it was before.

Brexit consumed all of Britain's political oxygen from 2016 to 2019. Covid-19 is consuming all of our mental capacity and economic wealth in 2020. In 2021, we risk returning to the stale old debate about Scotland's constitution. Before we fall into that trap, though, let us please examine our long-term future and the way we can position ourselves to win in the new world order. The world has changed enormously in the last 50 years. It will change even more in the next 50. We can already discern the global trends that will shape the future. The past is gone, for good or ill. The future is there to be won, if we have the wisdom to seize the opportunity.

As we, the authors, opened our minds to the opportunities and thought more clearly about the practicalities, we became much more optimistic about Scotland's potential. We have a shared conviction of a positive future for Scotland, assuming it can rise above risk aversion and a dependency culture. We tell our story – the way Scotland can win and thrive – with a blend of carefully researched factual writing, personal anecdotes, and fictional debates.

We conclude by framing the next stage of the conversation. How can we fund the transition? What leadership gaps do we need to fill? How do we fix the social divide; and how do we resolve the political stalemate?

Chapter 1

The Vision Emerges

"If you want to build a ship, don't drum up the men to gather wood, divide the work, and give orders. Instead, teach them to yearn for the vast and endless sea."

Antoine de Saint-Exupéry, French writer and pioneering aviator.

"Opportunity is missed by most people because it is dressed in overalls and looks like work."

Thomas Edison (1847 – 1931)

On a train in central Scotland, a debate opens up on the nation's future…

Haymarket station, 2020

"Doomed, we're all doomed" intoned Jim Fraser, as he squeezed into the seat his colleagues had kept for him on the crowded Edinburgh to Glasgow train.

"Hi, Jim, what catastrophe looms today?" asked Jack Jones, the junior analyst who had recently joined the team.

Jim slapped the morning paper down on the table. Three headlines competed for the reader's attention: 'Referendum date set,' 'Financial firms move south,' and 'Third Wave of Covid Looms.'

"Och, that's just *The Scotsman*, panicking as usual," said Arthur Wilson, the benign 'uncle' of the team.

"But I'm panicking too," Jim replied. "We could lose our jobs or have to relocate. If there's a referendum date set, that means Nicola thinks she'll win. And what future have we got in an independent Scotland? The financial services sector would collapse; or at best, go into genteel but terminal decline."

"A lot of people think that's what would happen if Scotland became independent," murmured Frank Pike, "but why should it?"

The three others glanced at him, and quickly switched to 'paying attention to the boss' mode. He had that pensive-and-interested look on his face that said he'd been thinking seriously about this, and that his thoughts would probably be worth listening to.

Pike was the team leader and, in his mid-thirties, the youngest senior partner in Caledonian Innovation Futures. He'd had the misfortune to go to one of the few Scottish schools that still had compulsory Army Cadets, and had got very, very sick of the inevitable 'Private Pike' jokes, particularly since, being tall and a bit weedy, he bore a passing resemblance to his fictional namesake. No one in the firm could work out whether it was bizarre coincidence, or a manifestation of a deep and subtle sense of humour, that his team all shared names with *Dad's Army* characters; and he wasn't going to let on. At work, he was professional and strait-laced. His Facebook profile suggested he had quite a different private persona; but he kept his private and business selves rigorously separated, to the point that his colleagues were not completely sure his Facebook profile even described the same person.

"So," he said, having checked that he had their undivided attention, and speaking quietly to reduce the risk of being overheard – you never knew who might be listening in on a conversation on a busy train. "Let's assume that Scotland does become independent. If other people view it as a threat, what should we view it as?"

The others looked at each other in embarrassment. Was this as simple as it seemed, or was it a trap?

"An opportunity?" ventured Jones.

"Absolutely right," assented Pike. "Now, what are some of the major trends that are going to disrupt our industry, and this part of the world, in the next 20 years?"

"We'll run out of oil?" suggested Jim.

"Hmm. I used to think so," said Pike. "There was a lot of misinformation around a few years ago. But there's still plenty of oil under the Scottish continental shelf, and we've got the technology to extract it. Still, I'm not sure that's going to be the limiting factor."

"Oh, I agree" said Jack. "The transition from fossil fuels to renewables and Green energy is definitely going to happen."

Jim frowned. "Who knows how quickly, though? The Arabs think they've got til the end of the century. Greta Thunberg tells us we should do it in ten years. The technology will take as long as it takes."

Arthur stroked his beard and looked thoughtful. "So, it'll happen, but we can't spot the timing yet. Folk who move out of oil too quickly will lose the opportunity to keep milking the cash cow; but the ones who hang on for too long will find themselves with stranded assets that'll be worth nothing."

Pike nodded. "It's very important to get into the game early and be well through the low carbon transition before the oil market collapses. That might happen quite suddenly, when the green alternatives become better and cheaper. It's hard to see oil being replaced as fuel for jet engines, and as chemical feedstock. But the economics will all change when cars go electric and the volume demand for petrol and diesel collapses; never mind the effects of any carbon tax, or fee-and-dividend scheme."

"I'm not so sure about aeroplane fuel," added Jack, who was up on these things. "There's going to be electric planes flying passengers between the Orkney islands by 2022. And you could have electric planes flying the breadth of Europe by the late 2030s."

The train pulled out of the station. Most of the passengers who'd boarded at Haymarket resigned themselves to standing all the way to Glasgow. No social distancing now. No gloves either, but at least some had masks.

"Right, that's one opportunity. What's next?"

Arthur cleared his throat and spoke slowly when he saw he had their attention.

"Well, even if the world could get to zero net Carbon emissions by 2030, which seems very unlikely, the arctic ice would continue melting for decades. The whole Arctic Ocean might be ice free in summer by 2050, or even earlier. Commercial ships are already getting through the Northwest Passage and the Northern Sea Route in summer. So I think the opening up of the Arctic sea routes is another big opportunity. Imagine if Scapa Flow became as busy a port by 2050 as Singapore is now!"

"Can I just check," asked Jack, "what exactly are the Northwest Passage and Northern Sea Route?"

"The Northwest Passage is the sea route across the top of Canada, from Newfoundland to Alaska. Franklin and his crew all died trying to find it. And the Northern Sea Route is the route from the Pacific to the Atlantic across the top of Russia. Scotland has large safe deep-water ports. We're perfectly placed to act as a container transfer terminal, where you take containers off big ships coming from the Far East and put them on smaller ships to take them to the different European and American ports."

"But we've no infrastructure for that sort of thing," Jim pointed out. "Our only serious container port is Grangemouth."

"That's why it's an opportunity – a huge one, if we tackle it the right way; though it would need a lot of investment," said Pike. "That's two. Any more?"

"Fintech?" offered Jim. He took pity on Jack when he saw the lost look on his face and translated. "Financial technology – software, so-called Artificial Intelligence, to help manage financial transactions. It's already a huge industry. There's a lot going on here in AI, data science and clever software generally. Put one of the world's top software centres in the same town as a major financial services hub, and what do you get?"

"O-ppor-tu-ni-ty," the others chorused, showing a potentially career-limiting disdain for one of the firm's core values.

"Yes," said Pike. "We almost missed the boat on Fintech, but fortunately one of our teams got in with the new Scottish Fintech Innovation Centre a couple of years ago. They're working on a lot of really interesting propositions. And of course, there's a lot of opportunity in other areas of new technology and systems integration as well – medical, smart cities, precision agriculture, things like that."

"Yes – high-tech healthcare is a big opportunity with the increasingly aging population," said Jim, looking pointedly at Arthur.

Pike suppressed a grin. "Good one. Any more?"

"Reforestation!" said Arthur, keen to move the conversation on.

"What!!??" chorused the others in unison.

"Trees?" laughed Jack. "They take thirty years to grow! How is that a good investment proposition?"

Jim managed to turn a laugh into a sneeze. Pike smiled.

"Well, several reasons," Arthur continued. "Scotland used to be almost completely covered with woodland. It got cleared for firewood, and then for building warships in the Napoleonic wars, and then for charcoal, and then to make room for sheep, and then for sport – grouse moors, and deer 'forests' that don't have a tree to their name. And now there are so many deer that in most parts of Scotland, the trees can't regenerate naturally – no natural woodland, just miles and miles of bog and heather."

Arthur paused. No-one spoke. Interpreting silence as interest, he carried on. "Now, one prospect is simply to earn carbon credits for growing trees to absorb Carbon Dioxide out of the atmosphere.

"A second is to use native timber as building material for modern carbon neutral houses. Using trees instead of bricks and concrete means you're carbon free before you start! And we should transform our construction industry and adopt the latest German factory build techniques here. One of the biggest causes of construction cost overruns is weather delays. With factory-built modules, you only need a few days of reasonable weather on site to get a house up and weathertight.

"And then, there's a whole lot of new agriculture techniques broadly called Agroforestry, which are supposed to give higher food productivity per acre than current farming methods and put goodness into the soil so you don't need chemical fertilisers. They don't keep ploughing up the land either, so more carbon stays in the soil instead of escaping into the atmosphere. Agro-forestry is more labour intensive than current farming methods, but that's not a bad thing if you've got lots of people all over the country needing good basic jobs. Modern industry simply can't provide the same number of jobs as the old industries did last century."

"Hmm," said Frank, deciding Arthur had finished his mini seminar. "Interesting. Any other ideas? However wacky?"

"Another opportunity," ventured Jim, "would be to try to reverse the brain drain, but I can't see how to do it. Ambitious Scots go overseas to get more challenge, and money, and to be where the big decisions are made. Scotland pays for their education and their retirement, and in between, they pay their taxes elsewhere. How does that make sense?"

"My older daughter's just a bit younger than you, Jim, and the younger one's just a bit older than you, Jack. Kirsti's in London and Eilidh's in Brussels. If we want ambitious Scottish kids to stay and flourish here, we've got to have good jobs at all levels," observed Arthur. "A living wage for basic jobs that allow everyone to make a decent living. Good and secure jobs for skilled workers and graduate professionals; and much more incentive to build big, high-quality Scottish companies. They should keep their headquarters here, instead of selling out to foreign multinationals as soon as the founders decide to cash in. Maybe a sovereign wealth fund, like we didn't set up when the oil came, but Norway did. And maybe getting other sovereign wealth funds and pension funds excited about investing here."

"So, there we are Jim," said Pike, "maybe we're not doomed after all. And actually" – he lowered his voice – "do not pass this on to ANYONE. The reason we're going to Glasgow this morning is to talk to a big pension fund – for a major oil company, believe it or not. They want to start shifting their investments from oil to renewables, now, big time, to protect their members in case oil goes sour sooner than their parent company was forecasting.

"Our opportunity is that most of the Edinburgh investment funds are happy to keep their clients' money in the old world they understand, as long as the clients keep paying their fees. Several of our teams are already going full steam ahead in renewables and green tech, and we have good client references. Because we're ahead of the game, this client is asking to set up a trial portfolio with a few percent of their fund. Everyone recognises it's a risk, so the deal has little downside, and everyone wins if it goes well.

"I'm glad we had this chat, because it's got you all into exactly the right frame of mind for today's meeting."

"That sounds good. And the longer-term stuff about how financial services might still prosper in Scotland, independent or not, sounds really hopeful. It would be great if we could achieve even just *some* of that. But could it ever work?" asked the cautious Arthur.

"Well, it's not easy," agreed Pike. "Lots could go wrong. It would need committed effort, enough money, good marketing, and a bit of luck. So, there's lots of reasons for not doing it, if you're not up for a challenge. But can we do it, if we set our minds to it? Of course we can!"

"Absolutely," said Arthur. "Remember our history! Scotland's golden age in the 1700s and 1800s! Smith, Hume and others led the Scottish Enlightenment, Glasgow was the second City of the Empire, more ships built on the Clyde each year than in the entire rest of the World. Scots leading the East India Company and much of the trade with China, Hong Kong and the Far East. Investment in the USA led by the Scottish Investment Trust movement led by the Alliance Trust out of Dundee. We've done it before - we can do it again. It's not fantasy, it's part of our history and it's within our capability. How do we re- kindle the spark?"

"Aye, you were there, were you, Arthur?" asked Jack, earning a glare in return.

"Interesting," said Pike – in a different tone this time, giving the word a completely different meaning – "so – wisdom first, then wealth. Scotland was skint in 1740, completely turned around a century later."

"How much of it could we do under the status quo, without a huge constitutional upheaval?" asked Jim.

Pike looked thoughtful. "I don't know. It's a good question."

Where are we and where should we go?

"Would you tell me, please, which way I ought to go from here?" asked Alice.

"That depends a good deal on where you want to get to," the Cheshire Cat replied.

"I don't much care where" said Alice.

"Then," said the Cheshire Cat, "it doesn't much matter which way you go."

"...So long as I get somewhere," Alice added.

"Oh, you're sure to do that, if only you walk long enough" said the Cheshire Cat.

Lewis Carrol, Alice in Wonderland

Let's try, just for the moment, to ignore the typical, hyper-active attention-seeking politicians, obsessively focused on projecting the right image, surviving the next hostile press release, outdoing their colleagues in the next cabinet reshuffle, and winning the next election. A time horizon of between a few hours and a few years.

Irresistible global trends are shaping and changing the world we live in. We can't control these trends, but we can recognise them and choose how to respond. Can we surf the trends to get where we want?

This is the question that we aim to address as we explore six of these major trends, one in each of the next six chapters.

In the context of each trend, we will attempt dispassionately to take stock of where we are now, and to look at the past to understand how we got here. Then, we will try to visualise the future we want for our grandchildren. We will imagine ourselves inhabiting that future, looking back at our route from our own present to understand what we 'had' to do to get 'here', and how we harnessed those global trends to help us.

Before delving deeper into our own vision for the future, it is useful to look briefly at four key factors that have combined over the past 50 years to bring us to this suspended state: politics, economics, the environment, and the pandemic.

Politics – and why we're ignoring it

Scotland could have a great future. It has the potential, as we aim to show in this book. But we're stuck. Politicians are so obsessed with the constitutional debate – Brexit, independence or not – that none of them seem to be looking ahead with ambition and vision to see what Scotland could be. This book is an attempt to shift the debate from being positive (or more usually negative) about politicians, to being positive about the future of Scotland.

In the 2014 referendum, Scotland voted 55% to 45% to stay in the United Kingdom. Some said, and many hoped, that this would settle the Scottish independence question for at least a generation.

The 2014 vision of an Independent Scotland included a good dose of optimism about oil revenues, and a commitment to a continuing currency union with the UK. Because neither of these was in Scotland's gift, risk-averse voters were unconvinced. Their misgivings seemed to be amply justified 18 months later, when the oil price slumped - in the very month independence would have happened if "Yes" had won.

Then came the British 2016 Brexit referendum, in which the UK as a whole voted to leave the EU, while Scotland and Northern Ireland voted to remain. This result was irreconcilable with the 2014 Scottish referendum vote to stay in Britain, influenced by the threats and promises from 'No' campaigners that 'only a no vote would keep Scotland in the EU.' The vision of Better Together proved to be a chimera - a failed promise of staying in Europe, being listened to in Westminster, and being generally better off for it. In reality, the country is even more divided politically. The pound has devalued with no tangible benefit. The economy was at best drifting in 2019 and is set to decline by a further 10% in 2020 thanks to the double whammy of Covid-19 and Brexit. And the fact remains that Scotland is being dragged out of the EU against its will.

The words Stephen Maxwell wrote in 2012[1] now seem profoundly prescient. "[Alistair] Darling invokes the risks of independence. He ignores the risks to Scotland of remaining in the Union. … It's not only change that carries risk; the status quo carries its share too."

The political question remains unresolved.

So we'll ask you, the reader: what constitutional arrangement do you think Scotland will have – in five years, after the next Holyrood and Westminster elections? – in ten year? – in 50?

How much would you be willing to bet on your guess being right?

We certainly wouldn't bet on it. That's why we are ignoring the politics and looking instead at long term global trends, which will shape our future over the next fifty years regardless of who happens to be in power. That is because a strategy which harnesses these irresistible global trends will be valid no matter what political structures we are operating under. The challenge to politicians is to show how their party's policies will best harness the global trends, for the benefit of Scotland and all of its people.

Economics

The old industrial communities in Scotland, in common with other parts of the UK, have suffered from the effects of a perfect storm – a series of structural problems that individually would have been manageable but taken together have left us stuck. The scene was set long ago, by Britain's overwhelming dollar-denominated war debt of WW2. Politicians demanded an 'export led boom' – no time for investment, just make anything we can sell. We didn't update our industries to compete effectively with rebuilt Europe and emerging Asia. Things started to slide in the economic crises of the 1960s and 1970s. In the 1980s, Thatcherism came like a tsunami and largely wiped out the remaining empire-era industry that had sustained communities for a hundred years. The oil boom and the promised Silicon Glen would solve all these problems. The late 1980s and 1990s was a calm that turned out to be the eye of the storm. The temporary economic upturn lasted about a decade; Silicon Glen turned out to be unsustainable, the banking crisis in 2007-8 knocked the stuffing out of the recovery, and we were back to staring at a hole in the central belt's wellbeing.

These basic structural problems created social problems that have not been solved from way back in the Thatcher era and before. Communities were demolished. Men lost their manual jobs, their dignity and standing in the community. Families were broken. The new towns provided housing but to a disconnected society. Older communities tinkered with their problems at the edges. High streets were gone, community centres declined. The best council houses were sold. There was no money to build new ones, nor to stop the older houses from deteriorating. Thatcherite Norman Tebbitt's hollow advice to the unemployed to "get on your bike to find new work" missed the point. There was no new work anywhere for many of the folk affected – and if there was, there was no affordable housing. No political party had realised that the scale of the damage would be so devastating: competition from smarter Japan, lower cost India and China, and the open access of Eastern Europe finished off our inefficient traditional industries – shipbuilding, coal, steel, cars, jute, linoleum. The ones that survived did so by drastic modernisation, improving efficiency, and shedding jobs in the process.

No political party in the last 40 years has really dealt with the fundamentals of Scotland's industrial decline. The consequences for the people who lost their jobs and their hopes for the future, and saw their communities collapse around them, are starkly illustrated by Darren McGarvie's book *Poverty Safari*[2] and his recent (late 2019) TV programmes.

The net effect of this is to have created three Scotlands: the many 'successful' folk with secure jobs, good incomes, good prospects and good lifestyles, often derived from oil and financial services; the folk who value a different form of 'success', and are content to keep out of the rat race and live within their means in beautiful places; and the 'left behind', particularly the young with no prospects in the city estates and smaller towns.

Many have been 'left behind'. Over half a million Scots, a tenth of our population, live in 'relative poverty,' of whom 100,000 are classed as destitute. A quarter of Scotland's children live in families classed as 'working poor' – with jobs that don't pay enough to make ends meet. 30,000 family units present as homeless each year. That's bad in itself; but worse, the poverty and social disintegration, the human stories behind these bald statistics, have caused intractable inter-generational health problems. The health problems won't go away by spending on treatment alone. To fix those health issues we need to tackle the root causes and give the 'left behind' different and better life prospects to prevent the damage happening in the first place.

That thinking requires a sustainable economic recovery to fund a social transformation. In that recovery, a much greater emphasis can be given to the wellbeing of the underprivileged. That's why this book focuses on economic opportunities: without them there will be insufficient wealth to restore the health and vibrancy of our people and our communities.

Environment

Another challenge to the established order comes from the new generation of environmentalists who emerged, big time, in 2018. The environmentalists, of course, are only the messengers. The real challenge comes from the immutable laws of nature! The environmental crisis that has been building up for thirty years or more is now well and truly upon us. Human society faces an environmental tsunami: not just climate change, but biodiversity loss, desertification, ocean acidification, and global pollution from excess fertiliser use.

This is both a challenge and an opportunity for Scotland. We have been highly dependent on fossil fuels since the 1960s; and the assumption of continuing oil wealth was one of the less stable planks of the SNP's independence pitch in 2014, as we have already noted. But we also have abundant, inexhaustible and readily accessible supplies of clean renewable energy. And every cloud has a silver lining: the arctic sea ice will continue to melt for decades even if humanity halts its greenhouse gas emissions in their tracks. This will open up new sea routes and new commercial prospects that Scotland is well placed to benefit from.

The wise oil states, such as Norway, Qatar, Saudi, UAE and Kuwait, invested in a Sovereign Wealth Fund, and are now using their oil wealth to prepare for the post-oil future. By contrast, since Britain used its oil wealth for debt repayment, extra consumption, Government revenue spending, and new infrastructure mostly in the south of the UK, Scotland does not have this buffer fund to call on. Nor will the future be kind to those countries that continue to invest in old-style infrastructure, traditional houses and patchwork transport systems. With that, then, the environmental question also brings us back to economic issues – where is the money going to come from to fund our transition to the post-oil future?

Pandemic

The unexpected Covid-19 pandemic hit every country in the world, and virtually stalled the world economy. This is causing serious problems for less resilient countries with already high debt levels. Italy is not alone. For Scotland, heavily reliant on oil, financial services and tourism, the economic impact is likely to be very hard. Oil has experienced a major double dip since 2015, and the three-way price war in early 2020 between the oil giants – USA, Russia and Saudi – has clobbered the small higher-cost producers such as Scotland just as the pandemic was starting. We can't rely on oil money alone to pay for our recovery from Covid-19 and our transition to a post-oil economy.

Tourism has also been battered. The 2020 Edinburgh Festival was cancelled for the first time since its launch in 1947. Our financial services sector is heavily reliant on the City of London – which, like the world's other financial centres, has been rocked to its foundations by the Covid-19 economic shut-down – and on the local Scottish economy, which was already struggling to recover from its long-term de-industrialisation before the new challenges appeared. Over 4,000 Scottish residents died directly due to Covid-19. Along with Britain, Scotland had one of the highest death rates in the world from the first wave of the pandemic.

In summary, Scotland has suffered a serious train crash because of the combination of a perfect political storm, a long economic decline, an environmental derailment, and a head on clash at high speed with a global virus.

So how do we pick ourselves up from this disaster, and what have we learned from the events that caused the crash? Is there an attractive future for the country? Can Scotland be turned around and be a winner again? Or is it, in the words of that infamous meme[3], too wee, too poor and too stupid to recover?

The worst thing for the country to do, after it recovers from this train crash, would be to return to the stale debate of 2014, when the vision for the country is expressed in political terms only. The second worst thing would be to make a half-hearted attempt to respond to the climate emergency, for example by repeating our failure, unlike Denmark, to create leadership in wind power. The third would be to be so scared of the impact of Covid-19 that we give up hope of being able to recover by our own efforts and simply depend on others to rescue us.

Politics consumes all the attention, but it is only the who and the how. We need to address the economic questions first. Where do we want to head for? What opportunities should we pursue to create sustainable and enduring wealth? Who for - for the one percent, or for the whole community? These are fifty-year questions. The debates on funding, social policy and politics are "how to get there" questions, of obsessive interest to politicians and journalists, usually framed and answered on a much shorter timeframe. Most politicians work on a time horizon of a few weeks, the next election at best.

So, the first big question, and the one we want to address, is: how can Scotland do well economically post Brexit, post Covid-19, and with the world starting to face up to the looming climate emergency?

Six opportunities to thrive

Fortunately, when you look through that lens, Scotland does have the potential to thrive in the new world of change. There are at least six big enduring opportunities for this small country to create the sustainable wealth needed to underpin the health and wellbeing of its inhabitants:

- focus on the opportunities presented by the inevitable melting of the northern Ice, reversing 1000 years of looking south – to England and France, and later to the Empire;

- capture wealth from the green transition, investing in renewable energy exports and technology, funded by the remaining years of oil returns;

- reverse the outrageous misuse, for 300 years, of its sparsely populated land;

- build on its historical medical strengths to create a more resilient, post Covid-19, small nation benefiting from medical science, smart health technologies and simpler medical systems;

- invest heavily in marine, renewable and Artificial Intelligence (AI) technologies, joining the so-called 4th Industrial Revolution and learning from the failed Silicon Glen initiatives;

- base future infrastructure on virtual cities, smart networks and environmental materials.

Making good use of these six opportunities will create the jobs and wealth we need to win in the new world.

We, a small country at the periphery of Europe, can partner with and learn from our successful Nordic cousins. Our vision of what a society should be like is similar to theirs, and we are likewise well endowed with abundant natural resources, and skilled, well-educated people.

This narrative, charting a 50-year journey into the future, is written by authors who have changed their minds on Scotland's potential, having looked to a future well beyond the politicians' short horizon. By re-examining Scotland's potential together, we have developed a shared belief in a positive future for Scotland, assuming it can break free from what many see as its growing risk aversion and dependency culture[4].

"No time for that, what about today's problems"?

You may already be asking, "This is all very well, but are you simply ignoring all the social and political problems that the nation is facing today?" The answer is, "No, we are not". We will deal with those critical issues later. We are very clear that, without adequate wealth fairly distributed, we will struggle to deal with those other matters. An economic turnaround is essential. Heaven forbid, however, that this becomes a narrow chase for economic growth alone or causes a further widening of the inequalities seen in the last 20 years. Our measure of success, as we will discuss later, is based on a number of measures of wealth and wellbeing, sustainability and resilience. We therefore welcome the recent shift that is emerging in many circles towards 'wellbeing economics[5]' and a shift away from narrow measures such as GDP per capita only[6]. This book, however, is focussed more on how to achieve tangible results over fifty years and less on the debate about how to measure them.

We remain interested in the traditional metric of Gross Domestic Product (GDP) per Capita, mainly because it allows useful international comparisons. But it's not the whole story, and if used as a single measure of success it will drive us to destruction. To get a better understanding of how wealth is distributed through the community, and how ordinary folk are doing, we looked at other indicators, such as the Gini index, which measures inequality; mean and median measures of asset wealth; and one or more of the various Happiness Indices. These reflect more appropriately the health, wealth and wisdom of a nation. We also need to restore and steward our natural environment – climate change is only one of several "planetary boundaries" already being violated by human industrial civilisation. Those familiar with Kate Raworth's Doughnut model[7] and the Ellen Macarthur Foundation's circular economy concept[8] will see where this might be heading.

In future publications we aspire to deal with the critical social and political matters, once the vision for sustainable wealth creation and stewardship is understood and debated fully.

Our vision is summarised in Chapter 8. The bases for that vision, our six key ideas, unfold in Chapters 2 to 7. Scotland can win and thrive in this new world. It has the natural resources and talents to turn itself around.

Our view – see what you think.

"We look to Scotland for all our ideas of civilisation." Voltaire (1694-1788), referring to the Scottish Enlightenment

"Skate to where the puck is going, not where it has been." Wayne Gretzky, Canadian ice hockey champion

References for Chapter 1

[1] Maxwell, Stephen. *Arguing for Independence – Evidence, Risk and Wicked Issues*, Luath, 2012/2013 p.179
[2] McGarvey Darren, *Poverty Safari*, Luath, Press 2018
[3] Apparently coined by John Swinney, and hijacked by the twitterati on both sides of the argument.
[4] See for example Carol Craig, *The Scots' Crisis of Confidence* (2nd ed'n.), Argyll Publishing, 2011
[5] https://wellbeingeconomy.org
[6] https://nationalperformance.gov.scot
[7] Kate Raworth, *Doughnut Economics: Seven Ways to Think Like a 21st-Century Economist* – Random House, 2018
[8] https://www.ellenmacarthurfoundation.org/circular-economy/concept

Chapter 2

Looking North

"The American dream is alive and well....and living in Finland"

Paul Krugman, Nobel economist.

"Vision without action is merely a dream. Action without vision just passes the time. Vision with action can change the world."

Joel Barker

Scotland needs to look North not South for the next part of its story. The melting of the Arctic sea ice will be one of the most significant world events of this century. It will open up a completely new sea route which will transform global trading patterns. Not only trading opportunities, but the region holds significant resources which will be developed by nine active nations who are already investing strategically in the region. With investment and commitment, Scotland can win its fair share of the resulting wealth, leveraging its considerable advantages – ideal location, enormous natural harbours – and its well-established marine industrial services sector. A new alliance with the successful Nordic nations, especially Norway, could benefit Scotland hugely in the long term.

A story of the North, in the present

In 1468 the daughter of the King of Denmark, Norway and Sweden married the Scottish king. Her father gave the Orkney and Shetland islands to Scotland as her wedding dowry. 550 years later, the islands still have a distinct Nordic identity. They also have a new confidence and prosperity, thanks to the money the Island Councils negotiated from the oil companies when the oil boom came in the 1970s.

The tiny pilot boat lurched horrendously in the confused waves, where the ocean swell, already jumbled by the currents of the notorious Pentland Firth, met the huge tanker's wake. The tanker's captain watched as the pilot boat gingerly approached the boarding ladder suspended near the tanker's stern.

Glad I don't have to do that, he thought, as the pilot stepped from the leaping deck of the pilot boat onto the boarding ladder, timing his move to perfection. With a surge of power, the pilot boat sprang away from the tanker, spray going everywhere. Once clear of the wake, it kept pace with the tanker, sheltered by the tanker's bulk from the worst of the waves rolling in from the Atlantic. The two vessels set course for the relative calm of Scapa Flow.

"Magnus Heddle, Scapa Flow Pilot, reporting Sir. Do I have your permission to take control of your vessel, and take her into Flotta Oil Terminal?" Magnus spoke formally, with only a trace of Orkney accent. The Singaporean Captain's English was excellent, but he wouldn't have understood a word of the broad Orkney dialect Magnus used with the crew of the pilot boat. (And, to be fair, neither would most mainland Scots.) Like most Orcadians, he spoke the local dialect with fellow Islanders, and switched to standard English with foreigners - which in his mind meant anyone not from Orkney or Shetland.

Magnus spent a few minutes familiarising himself with the ship he was now responsible for, and debated with the Captain and First Officer how they would bring the large vessel into the oil terminal. Once the plan was agreed, the First Officer took charge of the detailed movements of the ship through the Traffic Separation Zone, and the Pilot and Captain had time for a few minutes' conversation.

"What do people in Orkney make of this Scottish independence thing, Mr Heddle? Is it just fantasy, or might it really happen?"

"Aye, two questions there, and big ones!" replied Magnus. "Second one first: yes, it might really happen. Most Scots don't want to leave the European Union and are really angry about Brexit; and almost all of us are appalled at the political goings on in London. I often disagree with Nicola Sturgeon, but I have to say that since the Brexit referendum, she's about the only British politician who's understood what's going on and been talking sense. In fact, I think she's hardly put a foot wrong. When the other politicians talk complete bo... I mean, rubbish, she comes out with something considered and sensible. She seems to be thinking several moves further ahead than anyone else. Down in Westminster, our respected and revered Mother of Parliaments isn't doing so well now. I don't think Britain can survive Brexit, and certainly not without drastic political changes.

"But I'd want to be convinced that an independent Scotland ruled from Edinburgh would be better for us in Orkney. The Scottish Government wants to centralise and control everything it possibly can. In Britain, everything gets sucked into London; in Scotland, everything gets sucked into Edinburgh. We're still waiting for them to empower the islands as they promised in the 2018 Island Act. Lots of Scottish Government ministers came up here, lots of meetings, lots of nice words – promises but no empowerment. Orkney's transport links with the rest of Scotland are still a joke. The land transport connections with the Orkney ferries in Caithness are dreadful; and the flights are often delayed or cancelled because of bad weather.

"Some people here think that if Scotland gets independence from the U.K., then we should declare independence from Scotland. It doesn't make much sense - we really are too small to be a viable country. There's only 20,000 people living in Orkney, and about the same in Shetland. You'd need more than that just to run a civil service! But Scotland's another matter. We've about the same population as Singapore, with a lot more land area, and a lot more natural resources. We're less well placed as a centre of trade, but we've a great history of innovation of all sorts. So, if Singapore can do it, and Finland, and Norway, I don't see why Scotland shouldn't be perfectly viable as an independent country - if we choose to go that way. And, to be fair, last time there was a poll, it was less than 10% of us thought Orkney and Shetland should go independent from Scotland, or re-unite with Norway.

"But I've said enough. I really want to know what you think about it?"

"Well, Singapore had lots of problems when we were part of Malaysia; and we've done very well since we became independent in 1961. We're uniquely lucky because of our position in the world. Something like 25% of the world's sea trade comes through the Straits of Malacca, so it's only natural that Singapore has become the world's biggest container port. And we worked hard - very, very hard. We are five million Chinese and Indians, surrounded by 250 million Muslims, so we need to be able to defend ourselves, and to be as self-reliant as possible, in case we ever have serious disagreements with our neighbours. For example, we used to import most of our water from Malaysia. Now we don't need to anymore: every drop of rainwater that falls on Singapore is captured and used; and we can even export water to Malaysia, if they need it.

"But, of course, we try to be good neighbours, because it's far better to collaborate for mutual benefit than to argue all the time. And we've made Singapore a good place for international companies and for start-ups. Collaboration is in our DNA! We encourage R&D. Taxes are low. Our education is excellent. We value social cohesion, so crime is almost non-existent. There is low-cost unskilled labour, thanks to guest workers from Indonesia and Malaysia. And, most importantly, we Singaporeans work very, very hard. With all due respect, Mr Heddle, Scotland has a lot going for it; but you have allowed your formerly excellent education system to deteriorate; and your people don't want to work hard. Or at least, a lot of them don't.

"But, on the plus side, a threat to Singapore is an opportunity for you." The captain looked with some embarrassment at the stream of grey smoke spewing from the tanker's funnel. "Because of global warming, the arctic sea ice is melting. It looks almost certain that the Northern Sea Route across the top of Russia will soon be ice-free for most of the year. That will reduce the sea journey from China and Japan to Europe by something like thirty percent. That's over a week. And - oh, this has been a really interesting discussion, but we should probably turn our attention to our navigation duties - we see opening up in front of us the largest natural harbour in the North Atlantic. You've an area here similar to the whole of Singapore's harbour area. It would be an ideal container transfer port at the west end of the Northern Sea Route. Don't you think?"

"It's an enticing prospect" agreed Magnus. "Scapa Flow was full of ships in the two world wars. It would be great to see it full of ships again, for peaceful purposes.

"Right. Could you please alter course 30 degrees to port, and reduce speed to six knots?"

The present reality

Scotland is a small nation with limited financial resources, perched on the north-west edge of Europe. It is part of a United Kingdom that traditionally looked West, East and South for its success. But that could very well change soon.

For Scotland, the world can be turned on its head. No matter how clever we are as humans in targeting the climate crisis, there is one undeniable truth: the ice is going to melt north of Russia[1], and the Northern Sea Route (NSR), a new northern shipping trade route, is already opening up – we would expect it to be well-established by 2035. Given that, the next generation of Scots will witness a geographical revolution that will emulate the impact of the opening of the Panama and Suez Canals. Some estimate that this will reduce the trade flow through the Red Sea by at least half.

We will suddenly find ourselves at one end of a massive new trading route from Japan, China, Korea, and Russia to Europe and beyond. Northern Europe will see a growth in trade - a potential economic boom for Scotland, Denmark and other well positioned nations. Scotland will also benefit indirectly from the massive investment planned by the nine countries which have identified the Arctic as the most significant new region of economic development in the world: Canada, Norway, Iceland, Denmark, Finland, Sweden, Russia, USA and China.

How Scotland should prepare for this is not yet fully clear. Since the USA emerged as the major world economy, since Britain withdrew from East of Suez, and since London strengthened as a global financial centre, Scots have been attracted south and west. Two of the authors have lived this story over the last 40 years. However, the rallying cry for this vision is going to be to "think north" and invest in the economic boom that will ensue.

Scotland's significant advantages are apparent. Safe deep-water ports such as Scapa Flow in Orkney and Dales Voe in Shetland are well positioned to satisfy a large-scale demand for docking, maintenance, container transhipment, and other marine services. That, combined with potential West Coast oil development and the demand for specialised marine equipment, could stimulate new very long-term industrial growth – an important opportunity largely ignored so far by UK politicians, businesses, the media, and other institutions.

Not only that, but the Arctic is set to be a new frontier for a wide range of developments in trade and resources. Russia, Finland, Denmark, Sweden and Norway all geared up by 2016, to establish their policies and strategies to develop the region. China and the USA are jealous of the geographical position of those countries, and also of Canada and Greenland's equivalent position for the Northwest Passage. The two superpowers are figuring out how they can increase their involvement. If the Middle East was a centre of oil development and wealth creation for the last century, the North is going to become a similar economic hotspot for the next.

Scotland, though not in the Arctic region itself, is ideally positioned to benefit from this new northern passage and regional economic boom. Let's not allow southern countries to crowd us out or beat us to it.

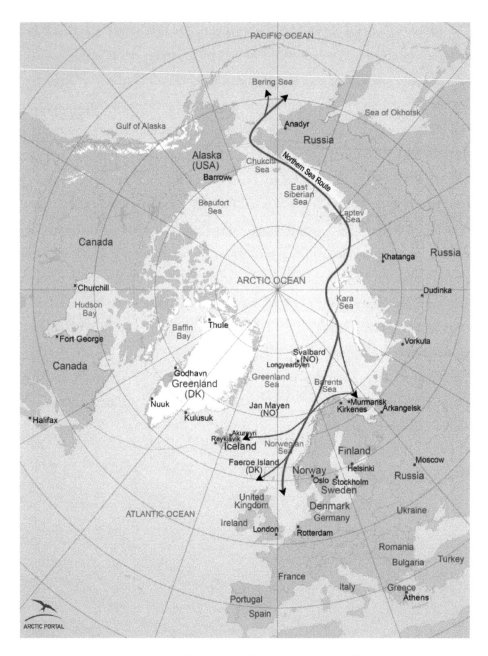

Map showing the Northern Sea Route, across the top of Russia.

The Arctic Portal is a non-profit organisation, under an international board of advisory directors, established to carry out outreach and communication on Arctic issues. Halldór Jóhannsson, Executive Director, has provided input for this book and kindly donated the image above.

The Future Potential

"Most investment firms don't even have the Arctic on their radar. Eventually they will."

Guggenheim Partners, 2019

Recent studies by the UK Government have been excellent on analysis but typically short on hard-nosed industrial strategy with financial backing. To quote the conclusions from one study:

"Future economic opportunities include capitalising on increasing Europe-bound traffic through the North Sea. The prospects of an ice-free Arctic have led to Stornoway Port Authority proposing their long-term vision to become an Arctic gateway hub in 20 years, due to their strategic location for European bound trans-Arctic shipping. In 2016, China's COSCO shipping company (one of the world's largest) sent five vessels through the Northern Sea Route (NSR), one of which delivered wind power equipment to the UK, becoming the third voyage to the UK via the NSR. Awarding the contract for the new Arctic research ship to UK shipbuilder Cammell Laird ensures that the UK retains its future readiness to construct specialist ice-class vessels. Arctic shipping technology providers typically supply services globally; currently there are only a very small number of these specialist technology providers, most notably in Finland." [2]

Building RRS Sir David Attenborough on Merseyside for arctic research, at a cost of £200 million, is a start - but what about a major investment in industrial ports and further arctic marine technologies for a 30-year future? Stornoway declaring that it has a vision for becoming an Arctic-focused port is excellent; but will it follow through with action, planning, commitment, money and marketing? Or will it go the way of most industrial policy in the UK and Scotland – half-hearted and fragmented? How about working with Glasgow, Forth Ports, Aberdeen, Orkney and Shetland to formulate a 50-year national Arctic strategy, with the backing of the Scottish Government, to create a major new industrial sector, based on maritime, marine energy, cold water and under-sea monitoring technologies?

We'll come back to this theme in Chapter 7 – you need critical mass to benefit from this sort of opportunity. It's disastrous for individual Scottish towns to compete against each other, when as a country we're competing against others with well thought out and strongly supported national strategies. We need to think of ourselves as one player, Scotland as one 'virtual city' of five million people, competing and at the same time collaborating with the other big international players.

There are hopeful signs. In September 2019, the Scottish Government published Scotland's Arctic Policy Framework[3]. It points out that Scotland's northernmost islands are closer to the Arctic Circle than they are to London, and that Arctic countries are important trading partners for Scotland. Shipping operations in the Arctic are on the rise, with growing international attention to the opening up of new water routes. Scotland has strong credentials to serve as a near-Arctic marine transport and logistics hub. Scapa Flow is the second largest natural harbour in the world – the largest in the North Atlantic – and has established itself as Northern Europe's preferred location for ship-to-ship transfer operations. Dales Voe in Shetland is the most cost-effective location for an ultra-deep-water port in the UK. This is particularly relevant to decommissioning of oil and gas facilities.

A critique by The Polar Connection[4] supports the argument that Scapa Flow has tremendous potential. It adds the slightly barbed comment that "Scotland could, therefore, **if willing to expand its offering** [our emphasis], be ideally placed to act as a sustainable hub for Arctic marine traffic. This opportunity has been recognised in Scotland's Arctic Policy Framework." Words are cheap, but serious planning and sustained effort, hard work and investment are required to make this vision a reality.

There is a major unresolved tension between commercial aspirations, and the Scottish Government's recent designation of much of Orkney's waters as Marine Protected Areas (MPAs), the highest level of EU designation for environmental protection.

Another challenge is the transport links between Orkney and the rest of the UK. The big container terminals such as Rotterdam are just parts of massive multi-mode logistics hubs, with excellent road, rail, air and river/canal connections to large hinterlands. Scapa Flow's unique advantage is as one of the most northerly, and the largest, of the safe harbours at the west end of the NSR. This makes it an ideal place for transhipping containers from large, probably ice-capable vessels traversing the NSR to smaller ones serving the different European and North American container terminals. Loads destined for central Scotland or

England or mainland Europe would continue their journey by ship to Grangemouth or Tilbury or Rotterdam. It would be a 'hub and spoke' operation with a very high level of automation. The first near-fully-automated container ports are already being built. Can we even imagine where the technology might be in fifty years' time?

The long-term economic potential is enormous. Some short-term tactics are also obvious. However, the UK is not one of the countries actively investing in the Arctic. Scotland will therefore have to establish a more coherent and ambitious twenty-year strategy to enter the game seriously, involving scientific cooperation, industrial positioning and geo-political relationship building.

The competition

Other neighbouring countries have already entered the marathon race. Norway has set a target of one new port as a support hub for the Northern Sea Route (NSR) by 2030 and three hubs by 2050. They have already secured the bulk of decommissioning work for retired North Sea oil and gas installations in both Norwegian and British sectors. Yet, their ambition is much wider and deeper, as part of their emerging strategy for a Sustainable Blue Economy in the Norwegian Arctic[5]. Their targets are to improve their ocean farming with better disease control, harvest from lower levels of the food chain in the sea, and prepare for mineral extraction from the seabed. At the same time, they propose to increase University courses for international students at UiT (the Arctic University of Norway, in Tromsø) on Arctic Technology in biology, geology and geophysics, and to create a new high-tech research centre for renewable marine energy. They have also set targets to increase Arctic Tourism and to create new cultural links, such as sports, with other Arctic countries.

Sweden started considering its options seriously in 2016. Among other conclusions and actions, it has established the need for specialised business incubators, such as their Arctic Business Incubator (ABI) in Lulea, improved mining technologies for the north, and much greater research on specialised Arctic technologies[6].

Finland, perhaps a little earlier in its thinking, has developed a similar mix of development expertise for the Arctic[7], with the design of specialised vessels, products and infrastructure and the promotion of winter testing services and winter navigation skills. They are working on various unmanned systems for remote and harsh environments. They have established a Team Arctic – a consortium of ten companies with expertise in energy, mining, marine, shipping and infrastructure. Like Norway, they also emphasise their offerings of specialised Arctic tourism experiences.

At the very least, if Scotland is late to become a leader in the Arctic development, then surely it can take the follower's attitude – "if you can't beat 'em, join 'em." Norway is one of the most active of the nine nations pursuing the Arctic. In any case, Scotland has an opportunity to cooperate with Norway on multiple fronts. It already has strong ties on oil and gas development, it plays a key role in marine security for the future, and as we will see later in this book, it has interests in expanding forestry, marine technology and marine agriculture. Furthermore, Norway has a surplus of sovereign money, whereas the UK has no such fund for long-term strategic investment. The other obvious partner for Scotland in terms of the Arctic is Canada, albeit more remote than Norway. Scotland's strong diaspora links to Canada could open up opportunities for future geopolitical and business initiatives that could be equally as important as the links to Norway.

Will the NSR turn out to be, not just the Northern Sea Route, but the New Silk Road?

China, classified as a near-Arctic country despite being 900 miles away, has already started its investment strategy in the region. It has invested in the Kvanefjeld Mining Project in southern Greenland, and is investing with Russia in the Yamal liquefied natural gas project[8], a key component of Beijing's emerging 'Ice Silk Road.' China opened a research station in Iceland in 2018 to study space weather[9]. It has another one in Norway's Svalbard Island, and it signed an agreement with Russia for a joint research centre[10] to forecast the ice conditions of the Northern Sea Route and provide recommendations for Arctic economic development[11]. No wonder Trump has offered to buy Greenland from Denmark. The geopolitical game between the USA, Russia and China has already started, big time, and the stakes are very high. The Middle East conflicts are about to be replaced by the geo-political 'Scramble for the Artic' or the 'New Cold War'. White army suits replacing the desert khaki as the uniform of choice. We owe it to ourselves not to miss out on the most significant geographical change to our world for the next three generations, right on our doorstep.

"Whoever has control over the Arctic Route will control the new passage of world economics and international strategies"

Professor Li Zhenfu, Dalian Maritime University, 2018

Nordic synergies and precedents

There is a second excellent reason for Scotland to look north rather than south. Sweden, Norway, Denmark, Finland and Iceland have all found a way to be highly successful as small nations. Pick your measure. According to the wealth index (GDP per capita) and the equality index (GINI measure), the happiness index and the investment levels in R&D, these countries are more successful than the UK, Germany, the USA, Japan and Korea.[12] [13] [14] [15]

The six charts after this section show how each of these Nordic countries is positioned in the world league, compared with other major countries including the UK. These are imperfect measures of health, wealth and wisdom, just a snapshot of success. However, they tell a similar story to the more complex (and perhaps less easily understood and compared) measures such as the Human Development Index[16] and the Scottish Government's National Performance Framework[17]; and they are representative of performance throughout the last decade, at least until Covid-19 hit in 2020. We expect these countries to recover better than most from the latest crisis. They certainly recovered well from the last banking collapse in 2008.

In terms of GDP per capita, which is a measure, albeit crude, of a country's generation of short-term wealth, Norway has done well from its major oil and gas finds, whereas Iceland had to work extremely hard to recover from the banking crisis of 2008. Denmark, Sweden and Finland have consistently beaten Germany, the UK and France in creating wealth. However, a slightly different picture emerges from looking at the wealth accumulated by the population over time.

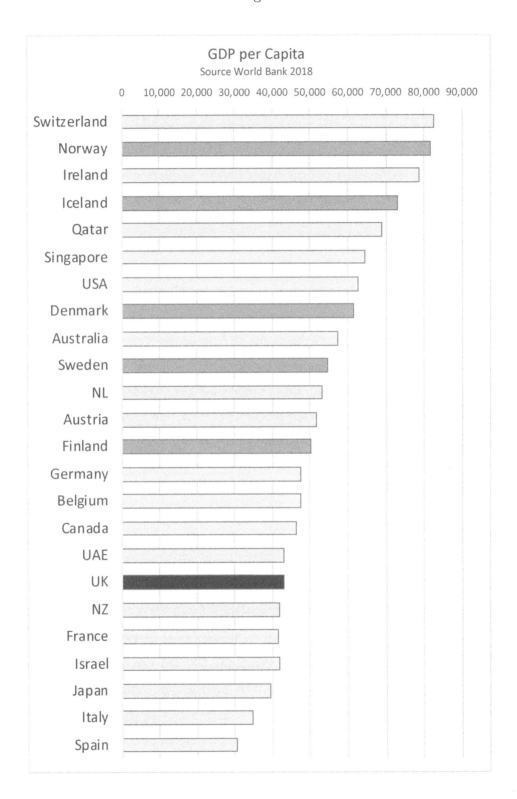

One measure of wealth accumulation is the mean wealth per adult. The Nordics are again in good positions, but, apart from Iceland, they don't do so well on this measure. The property wealth of the big European cities and their pattern of asset investment compensates for their countries' lower GDP per head. Thus, they are positioned above the Scandinavians and towards the top of the wealth league. Some argue that this property and asset wealth has caused people in countries such as Britain to become complacent, even lazy, at generating real non-asset wealth. Perhaps that is the case.

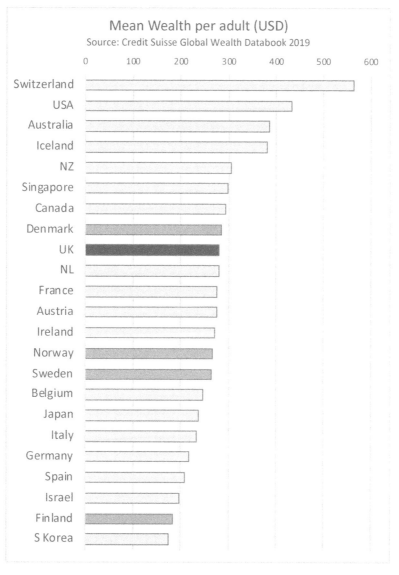

This difference is even more obvious when looking at the median wealth per adult which is more representative of the ordinary person rather than skewed towards richer people in less equal societies. The Scandinavian countries are near the bottom of our sample of wealthy countries by this measure.

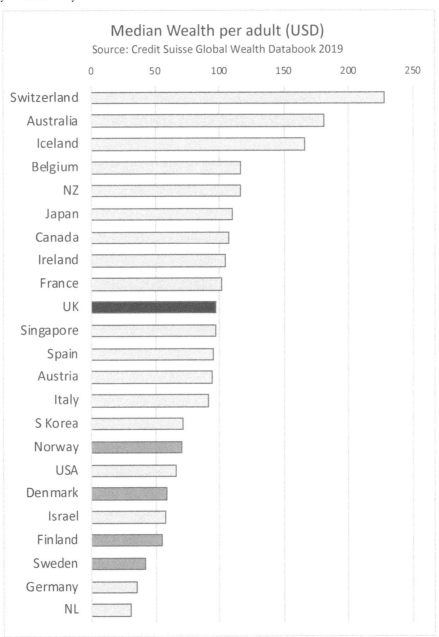

That leads us to another measure, the so-called Gini or Inequality Index. This is a measure of how equal a society is. If it's zero, everyone is equal. 100 denotes the highest possible inequality - one person has all the wealth. The five Nordic countries are all in the top seven of the world equality league. Sweden is particularly proud of being number one. This is one of the reasons they believe they have a stronger society than most other countries, particularly the unequal USA, Japan and Russia, and the less equal France and UK. (Chart 2D). Despite this, the Nordics remain worried by the worldwide trend to greater inequality.

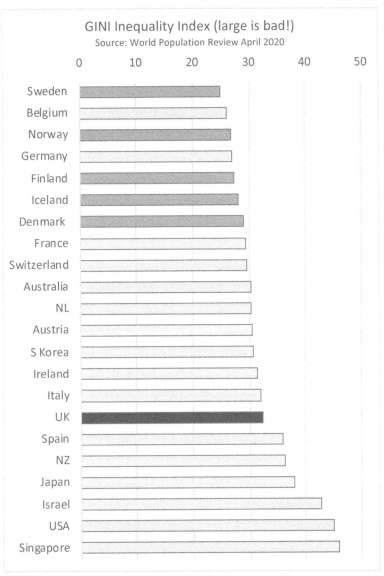

When one looks at these countries with a wider lens, the small Nordic nations at the periphery of Europe again come out particularly well. The Nordics top the world league of the World Happiness Index, which covers a wide range of economic, political and social measures. Only the Netherlands and Switzerland, another two small countries, separate the five Nordic nations.

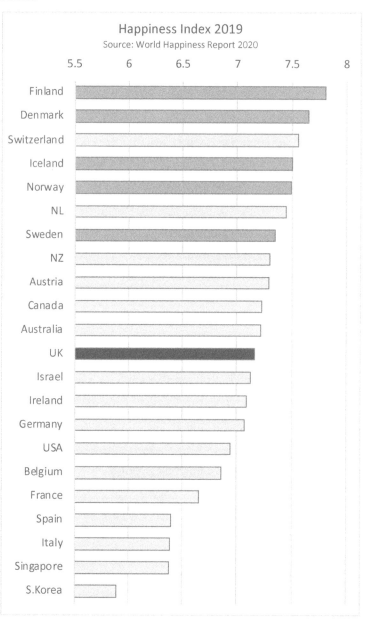

Finally, in case you might think that these societies are simply exploiting their past success, the last measure, of R&D per capita, demonstrates that they are investing heavily in their own future. Because it's a very useful comparison, we have placed this chart beside the one for GDP. We will come back to this in chapter 6. Scotland needs to double or triple its Research and Development to have any hope of matching Finland, Sweden, and Denmark. Britain (1.72%) has fallen down the investment table, now below most of its European peers apart from Spain and Italy, and well below Japan, Korea and China. Iceland is 2%[18]. Norway's position just above the UK is, as the Chinese proverb would have it, 'interesting.' We expect to see that change.

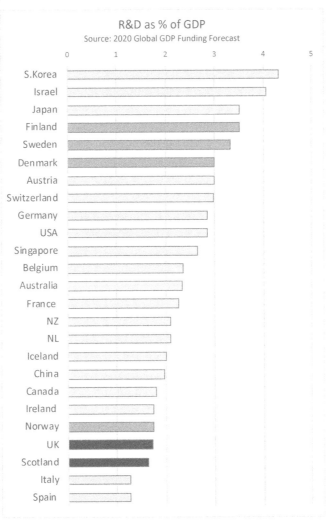

Notes to charts:

GDP is Gross Domestic Product, a measure of wealth creation.

"Mean" is the statisticians' word for "average".

Median" is the value that half of the population has more than, and half the population has less than. Also called "50ᵗʰ percentile". The median is almost always less than the mean.

Gini is not an acronym! It's named after its inventor, Italian statistician Corrado Gini.

The Nordics – reasons to be cheerful!

Nordic Horizons, an ad hoc voluntary organization led by Lesley Riddoch, studied the reasons why the Nordic countries each provide excellent, though not perfect, analogies for Scotland to consider[19]. Every person in Scotland should understand why the Nordics' superior performance has occurred. Scotland is neither too small nor weak to better itself. In fact, we could – and should – perfectly well follow their example.

Let's take the case of Sweden, a country that has experienced a steady rise to success over the last 150 years. Johan Norberg offers an interesting view of Sweden's transition from the poverty of the 1850s to today's wealth in his 2013 article, "How did Laissez-Faire make Sweden rich?"[20] Sweden implemented early liberalism in society and business in the 1800s, deregulated the guilds to allow innovative start-ups, and implemented land reform early and successfully. It established highly efficient trading relationships and exports, creating large and successful companies, and joining the Anglo-French free trade zone in the second half of the 1800s. It was, effectively, the first common market.

Sweden built world-leading businesses based on forestry and wood products, avoided the two disastrous World Wars, recovered from a bad period in the 1970s which Norberg attributes to overdoing socialism, and recently invested in technology, entrepreneurialism and trading. No utopia, but a good role model for Scotland. It took Sweden 150 years. We hope to do it in 50!

Conversely, Finland found it more difficult to succeed but made the best of its more limited resources through hard work, forestry and wood-based trading, investing in electronics at the right time, and a world leading education system. Scotland will have to work similarly hard at its opportunities. Denmark exploited its perfect location in Europe for trading and shipping, its coastline, used its excellent agricultural resources and skills, found oil and gas, and invested in wind technology. Scotland is also well positioned for the new trading route and for investment in wind and wave power. Norway lucked out with oil and gas, had the wisdom to invest the wealth for a post-oil future instead of indulging in a consumerist spending spree, and now has one of the world's largest sovereign wealth funds.

In spite of their high taxes, Norway is home to more billionaires per head of population than the UK, as is Sweden – according to Wikipedia, Sweden is 9th in the world rankings, Norway 11th, and the UK 24th. The pejorative labelling of these countries as socialist states is misleading. Strong market economies with substantial social programmes, high levels of wellbeing and less inequality would be a better description. The lesson is that higher but fair taxes don't necessarily drive billionaires away from a country that's a good place to live, work and invest in. This matters: Scotland is 'home' to more than twice its share of Britain's billionaires.

Norway is also allowing its woods and forests to recover. A landscape ripped bare by logging a hundred years ago, like Scotland's more recently, is now returning to flourishing mixed woodland.

Finally, the Nordics (apart from Sweden), along with other smaller nations around the world such as New Zealand, Singapore, Taiwan, Estonia, Latvia and Lithuania, seem to have done very well in the societal control of the Covid-19 virus. Perhaps Scotland can learn lessons from these nations about improving its health as well as its wealth and wisdom. Time will tell.

Wisdom came first

Anderson and Björkman's book *The Nordic Secret* offers another perspective on the Nordics' success[21]. As the Danish and Swedish empires declined in the eighteenth and nineteenth centuries, Nordic societies had to adapt to a new reality.

Today's unique combination of economic and social success didn't come by chance. Norway, of course, benefitted hugely from finding oil, and Sweden stayed out of the large-scale destruction of the second world war, but two quotes from the book highlight that their success is based on much more.

"The Nordic and Swiss histories have shown that good economies develop from responsible self-governing and self-authoring people, who can self-motivate."

"Rather than focussing on the economy, we should focus on the people, and let them take care of the economy when they are rounded and ready."

One part of the 'Nordic Secret' is certainly shared with Scotland: the 'Protestant work ethic.' Scots of the authors' and previous generations had the 'protestant work ethic' drummed into them. Another part was the wisdom of the Scandinavian elites of two centuries ago, who understood that, if societies were to become better and more cohesive, individuals at all levels, from richest to poorest, *'needed a richer and more complex inner world... to develop a sense of responsibility towards self and society.'* Some of this is achieved through a rich family and community life. Some of it is developed by a suitable education system. But learning doesn't stop when we leave home, or school, or university. Learning is a lifelong pursuit.

A book published in 2006 analysed a then-recent survey of work patterns in 15 EU countries[22]. Nordic countries scored well above the European average for workers in 'learning organisations' – characterised by a high degree of individual autonomy in work rate and working methods, learning new things at work, complex tasks with a high level of problem solving, and responsibility for the quality of one's own work.

In the Netherlands, Denmark and Sweden, over 50% of jobs were characterised as having a 'learning organisation' context. For the UK, the figure was 34.8% and for Ireland,

24%. Scotland was not reported separately but has been estimated[23] at 30%, between the UK and Ireland.

People in 'learning organisation' jobs are claimed to have a clearer sense of purpose and agency in life, better self-respect, better mental health, and to be 'less prone to the excesses of consumerism, materialism, alcoholism and other addictions, and hyper-individualism.' A society of such people has more social cohesion.

We conclude that an important part of the 'Nordic Secret' is the workplace – jobs and organisational structures that facilitate, or indeed require, continuous learning. Nordic countries apparently have nearly twice as high a proportion of such jobs as Scotland. Maybe that's the most important change?

And don't forget Ireland!

In addition to learning the tough lessons from the Nordics, Scotland can also learn more from its small neighbour, Ireland. Ireland has climbed the wealth league (GDP per capita) amazingly to become fifth in the world in GDP per capita terms, exceeding the USA which is 10th. A lot of this success was triggered 60 years ago by the famous civil servant, Thomas Kenneth Whitaker, the so called 'Architect of Modern Ireland'[24]. There is, however, a major question about whether this country is a good model for Scotland. Probably not. Ireland's GDP measure is inflated by money passing through the books of the big multinational companies based there. Gross National Income (GNI), a more meaningful measure of personal wealth, is merely good, not exceptional. Ireland has low corporate tax, low technology, low forestry, poor carbon footprint, low R&D, and lower levels of happiness and equality than its Scandinavian peers.

Still, Ireland is definitely a good model for Scotland in at least three respects. Its greater investment in music, language, arts and crafts has increased the cultural wellbeing of the nation. Its world diaspora is phenomenal, beating all small nations including Scotland, hands down, especially within the USA; and it has shown unrivalled guile in attracting foreign investment, particularly from Germany and the USA.

Scotland has been strongly aligned to a country, England, that is 10 times its size, looks south not north, and still wants to be a first-rank world power. The UK's continued search for a role post empire with the larger nations of China, India, Germany, Japan, USA and Russia does little for Scotland's specific interests in the North with the likes of Norway or Canada. As a small nation, it's time for us to "look north young person, not south." It's time to think that small is beautiful, not big.

A story of the North – 2070

Magnus Heddle's son Rognvald was bringing a container ship into Scapa Flow after its journey through the Northern Sea Route from Shanghai.

Rognvald went to nautical college in Shetland, and worked his way up through fishing boats, ferries, coasters and intercontinental container ships until he got his master's ticket. Then his father was coming up to retirement, and his job as a Scapa Flow pilot was advertised. Rognvald applied, and was thrilled when he was offered the job. To begin with, he had the excitement of jumping onto ladders from small boats and standing on the bridge of foreign ships bringing them through the same waters his father had worked for so many years. Then, new technology was introduced to make the pilots' job easier and "improve productivity." Now aged 50, Rognvald was able to do the whole of his job from a comfortable leather chair, with a panoramic view of Scapa Flow.

He glanced up from his screen to look at the real world. Scapa Flow was crowded with container ships and cranes. The curator at the Navy museum in Hoy had been in the control room on an open day and told him it was busier than it had been since World War One. But all the ships and cranes were dwarfed by the backdrop of the tree-clad hills of Hoy – and that was another change from his dad's time! Hoy used to be bare moorland, grazed by a few sheep. The 2020s saw a huge effort to stop over-grazing by sheep and deer to allow Scotland's woodlands to regenerate. Its success was due at least in part to the crude but inspired marketing slogan "save a tree – eat a deer." Venison sales rocketed, the deer population dropped by 80% in ten years, and most of Scotland was now covered in forest.

One of Rognvald's sons worked at the battery of wind farms on the west side of Hoy, where the wind blows strong and steady, and the small trees clinging onto the hillside don't disrupt the airflow through the wind turbines. The wind farms, now seriously ageing, were being pushed to the limits of their capacity to cope with the continual expansion of the marine port. His other son and his daughter worked at the airport, buzzing with the latest fleet of electric commuter aircraft that linked Kirkwall with Inverness, Aberdeen, Glasgow, Edinburgh, Lerwick, Bergen in Norway, and Torshavn in the Faroes. His wife was a manager in one of the agroforestry complexes on the island that had been established during the 2040s. She was responsible for a new agricultural pilot programme, a collaboration with the Agrotechnology Department of the University of the Highlands and Islands.

The captain of the ship Rognvald was controlling hailed from Shanghai. He had minimal English, and Rognvald's Orkney accent was much broader than his father's had been when he was in "professional" mode; but the two could communicate perfectly, thanks to the Hypertel® link that was established when the ship reached the outer controlled zone. There, several things happened that seemed like magic. Electro-magnetic coils powered by the strong tides in the Pentland Firth drew the ship along the desired course, with no need for the ship to use its own engines or steering. The engines stayed on standby in case of emergencies. The Hypertel® link allowed the captain and the pilot to communicate at the level of concepts rather than language, so each could "think" in their own native language. This actually resulted in better communication than in the old days, when everyone spoke in English, though with variable fluency and clarity.

When the electro-magnetic guidance coils were first introduced, the pilots were expected to sit and watch the system, and only intervene if the automatic system stopped working. After many months of incident-free operation, with the pilots getting increasingly bored and demotivated, there was a very near miss. A tug towing a marine energy system was crossing in front of an incoming tanker. The artificial intelligence guidance system controlling the tanker failed to understand what was happening and just gave up. A buzzer went, to alert the pilot to intervene and save the situation. It took more than a minute for him to work out what was actually happening, and another minute to slow the ship and achieve an emergency turn. A collision was only avoided by a few metres. Of course, it had to be the pilot's fault!

However, the pilot's union hired an expert witness, who ran a number of simulations, proving that with the information presented by the system, many human operators would not have avoided a collision. The automatic guidance system was switched off, and the pilots went back to the old ways with their boats, until new protocols were developed, using Hypertel® to link the pilot and the ship's captain, and keeping the pilot fully involved in controlling the ship at all times.

Rognvald didn't have much to do while the ship was conducted through the Traffic Separation Zone by the electro-magnetic coils. He was only half concentrating on controlling the ship, the other half of his mind occupied with memories of the dramatic events of 15 years ago. He came fully back to the present when the ship came out into the wide and bustling Scapa Flow harbour. He brought the ship into its berth, assessing the hazards, controlling all the different parts of the system, and communicating with the captain, all by just thinking. As he completed the manoeuvre, a thought flashed through his head. *If only my family were this easy to orchestrate, life would much easier! A family Hypertel®, now there's an idea.*

References for Chapter 2

[1] British Antarctic Survey. *Past evidence supports complete loss of Arctic sea-ice by 2035*. ScienceDaily, 10 August 2020. <www.sciencedaily.com/releases/2020/08/200810113216.htm>.

[2] Future of the Sea: Implications from Opening Arctic Sea Routes, Dr Melia, Prof Haines and Dr Hawkins, July 2017 UK Government Publication

[3] Scotland's Arctic Policy Framework, Scottish Government, September 2019. Open Government Licence v3.0 https://www.gov.scot/publications/arctic-connections-scotlands-arctic-policy-framework/

[4] https://polarconnection.org/scotland-marine-innovation-arctic/

[5] Sustainable Blue Economy in the Norwegian Arctic, June 2019. Written by DNV GL for the Centre for the Ocean and the Arctic

[6] Sweden's Arctic Strategy - An Overview, April 2019, The Arctic Institute, Nima Khorrami

[7] Finnish Prime Minister Office, March 2017, Action Plan for the Update of the Arctic Strategy

[8] CGTN.com, *Second phase of Russia-China Yamal LNG project enters operation,* 11 Sept 2018

[9] The Arctic Portal, *China-Iceland Arctic Observatory formally opened,* 18 October 2018

[10] High North News, *Russian and Chinese Scientists to Establish Arctic Research Center,* 15 April 2019

[11] Wired.com, Russia's Bid to Exploit Gas Under the Stunning Arctic Tundra, April 2019

[12] Various measures of GDP per capita can be found. IMF figures for 2018 have been used for this reference. The World Bank 2017 has slightly different measures but similar outcomes. The USA CIA agency again has slightly different numbers but again similar

[13] GINI Index by Country, World Bank Estimate 2017

[14] World Happiness Report 2019

[15] World Bank Open Data R&D per capita and as a % of GDP

[16] http://hdr.undp.org/en/content/human-development-index-hdi

[17] https://nationalperformance.gov.scot

[18] Knoema.com, World Data Atlas > Iceland, 2018 figure.

[19] Lesley Riddoch and Eberhard Bort, McSmorgasbord, Luath Press, 2017

[20] https://www.libertarianism.org/publications/essays/how-laissez-faire-made-sweden-rich

[21] Andersen and Tomas Björkman (2017) *The Nordic Secret: A European story of beauty and freedom.* Stockholm: Frit Tanke Förlag https://www.nordicsecret.org/; See also Jonathan Reams, *The Nordic Secret – What can we learn?* – Integral review, August 2018, Vol 14, No. 1

[22] Lorenz & Valeyr, Organisational Forms and Innovative Performance: a comparison of the EU-15 – Chapter 6 of book Lorenz and Lundvall (eds.) How Europe's Economies Learn: Coordinating competing models, Oxford University Press.

[23] Personal correspondence with Jim Mather, August 2020.

[24] https://www.irishtimes.com/life-and-style/people/tk-whitaker-obituary-1.2930820

Chapter 3

Reforesting the Wet Desert

"A nation that destroys its soils destroys itself. Forests are the lungs of our land, purifying the air and giving fresh strength to our people"

Benjamin Franklin

Scotland has underused and misused its natural resources, preserving its land for the benefit of a few and to present an image which, because of the decline of its wealthy industrial base since WW2, it can no longer afford. Better to use the land for a large-scale expansion of forestry and grow our wood-based economy to 3% of our GDP, creating over 25,000 new rural jobs and a large new export business. The aim is to triple the forestation from 18% to 60% with the right balance of commercial forestry, rewilding and agro-forestry.

Where have all the trees gone?

It was Saturday 21 September 2019. Edinburgh sparkled under the intensely blue sky, every detail pin sharp in the clear autumn air. Nature didn't care that British politics was in meltdown. We fled Brexit and drove north, to join a friend completing his second round of the Munros, on Mount Keen in Angus.

As we passed Kinross, fantastical wraiths of cloud drifted over Loch Leven and hid the lower slopes of the Lomond Hills. Turning off the A90 near Forfar, we drove into low cloud, and our attention turned to the closer landscape. Glen Esk is a mix of deciduous trees and conifers, of relatively natural woodland and organised planting. Around the mature trees, young saplings grow on any scrap of land where they're protected from marauding sheep. Any nook of spare land is occupied by young trees and too many plant species to count.

We assembled in the car park and walked towards Mount Keen. We passed through the last gate, and suddenly the landscape changed. A heather monoculture, wide open vistas, bare hills, the occasional alternative monoculture of a conifer plantation, and scorched squares of moorland burnt to allow young heather to regrow to feed grouse. Not a naturally propagated tree, and scarcely an animal or bird, to be seen.

The path led us for an hour of pleasant walking on the flat, then at a comfortable gradient up the side of a deep valley. Occasional "baa" sounds reached us from below. The sheep were almost invisible, as they searched out succulent morsels of green plants among the deep thick woody heather. The "baa-s" explained everything. Young trees didn't stand a chance.

Scotland – a wet desert…

We like to think of Scotland as a country of natural beauty; of the Highlands as a wonderful wilderness of heather hills and unspoilt glens. But this is factually wrong – a comforting myth that shields us from a bitter reality. Ecologically, Scotland is a man-made landscape, stripped of its goodness and of many of its people by centuries of various modes of human over-exploitation.

This line of argument goes back to Frank Fraser Darling, a young English scientist who arrived in Scotland in the 1930s, making his name with iconic books describing his experiences. In 1950, the Secretary of State for Scotland commissioned him to conduct a thorough assessment of the Highlands. His review completed, however, Darling was deliberately muzzled, for his shocking findings didn't fit the vested interests of the estate owners. The notion that "Humans are part of Nature, not just its keepers" got him into real trouble, just as it might today.

Yet, what Darling had to say is of the uttermost importance. He characterised the Highlands of Scotland as a "wet desert", asset-stripped by long periods of sheep farming (the "woolly locusts"), deer breeding, and "vermin elimination" – the culling of natural predators, such as eagles, polecats, weasels, and red kite. In spite of being illegal since 1954, raptor persecution sadly continues to this day. The aesthetically pleasing heather was a weed that killed other vegetation. The dense rubbery peat locked away the nutrients needed to create a better environment. The landscape was empty of trees, woodland ants, and worms, crucial for biodiversity. The addiction of killing deer and grouse to put trophies on walls had contributed to the Highlands becoming a desert, perhaps more colourful than the sand dunes of Saudi Arabia, but barely more productive. No wonder the Highlands are, with honourable but mainly small-scale exceptions, largely empty of people and devoid of sustainable economic activity.

The infamous Highland Clearances contributed considerably to the depopulation of the Highlands, but were not the only cause. The Highland ecology was already too depleted to support the growing population with the subsistence agriculture of the time. The crisis was brought to a head by three additional factors: changes in ownership structures following the '45 rebellion; Enlightenment thinking that farming could and should be 'improved', and that subsistence crofter should be swept aside to make way for new more productive farming methods; and also thanks to the Enlightenment, the breakthroughs in science and engineering that led to the rapid growth of labour-hungry industries in the central belt. So as the Highlanders (and Lowland country dwellers too) fled destitution, famine and the clearances, they found that North America and Scotland's newly industrialised central belt were opening their welcoming arms.

Not many Scots realise that Norway lost as much of its population to emigration as Scotland in the 19th century, with no coercion at all. In those days, subsistence farming in the northern extremities of Europe really wasn't much fun. As ever, those with the 'get-up-and-go' got up and went, to seize the opportunities they were offered with both hands.

Two centuries later, the highly profitable large-scale sheep farming that was established after the clearances has itself degenerated into subsidised, smaller-scale sheep farming and crofting. Forty percent of our subsidised sheep are exported. The abundant and variegated game bags of the shooting estates in the late 19th century have been reduced significantly – in numbers and particularly in diversity – by over-shooting. Grouse bags are going up again now, only thanks to the use of medicated grit to deal with the parasitic worms that infest unprotected grouse.

And at the same time, in the central belt, the collapse of the job-rich shipbuilding, car manufacturing, coal mining and steel making industries, and the drastic shrinking of the defence industry, led to a decline in wealth of a large segment of the population, and a rise in poverty and social degeneration. History repeats itself. We owe it to that devastated section of society to find a better way to restore, steward and use our natural resources to stimulate the economy. Otherwise we may well see another round of population decline, this time from urban clearances.

The idyllic image of beautiful but empty Scotland can no longer support the needs of the people who inhabit the land. In other words, "You can't live on a view!" Better land-use has huge potential to improve the environment, increase biodiversity, reduce our carbon footprint, and create more jobs in rural areas. Only 28% of Scotland's land is fully utilised economically. The figure for Sweden, Denmark and Finland is in all cases over 70%[1]. This wet desert is an economic, environmental and social tragedy.

* * *

Too few people realise the real reasons for the demise of the land, even though this is a crucial point. Forests became re-established in Scotland after the last Ice Age. Five thousand years ago, Scotland's woodland cover reached as far as Orkney and Shetland. Then, by Roman times, early agriculture and a cooler, wetter climate halved the area of woodland. In the early industrial age, the remaining woodland was heavily exploited, and by 1900, only 5% of Scotland was covered with trees[2].

Efforts to restore tree cover were interrupted by two wood-consuming war efforts. Since then, thanks to the commitment of the Forestry Commission[3] and private landowners and, more recently, the Scottish Government, woodland has been brought back to cover about 18% of Scotland, and forestry now contributes about one billion pounds, or 0.8% of Gross Value Added (GVA), to Scotland's economy[4].

The Scottish Government has created a ten-year action programme[5] with the aim of moving from 18% forestation to 21% by 2032. But that is nowhere near enough. Reforestation is not only one of the biggest opportunities for carbon capture and biodiversity that Scotland can offer the world right now, but it could also triple forestry's contribution to the economy with little new technology investment. Sixty-nine per cent of Sweden's land is forested. Forestry accounts for 2.9% of its economy, over 60,000 direct jobs, 200,000 indirect jobs, and substantial exports of forestry and wood products.[6] Agriculture accounts for a further 2%. Finland has 4.3% of its economy based on forestry, New Zealand 3%.

Scotland has room for at least 5 billion more trees – good for the economy and the environment simultaneously, so long as we plant the right tree in the right place and for the right reason.

The UK is the fifth largest importer of wood in the world, spending £8 billion a year on those imports and with a net import imbalance of £6.2 billion. Sixty per cent comes from Scandinavia, mainly Sweden and Finland. If most of the less productive farming area of Scotland were converted into much needed forestry, the Scottish industry could be tripled to about 3% of GDP, displacing UK imports and providing a major stimulus to jobs – potentially a further 35–50,000[7] scattered throughout Scotland. In 2011, a Scottish Forest & Timber Technologies report identified that over 33% of Scottish land is relatively unconstrained and suitable for additional commercial forestry[8]. A further large area would be suitable for 'conservation woodland,' unmanaged wild woodland which would be of little value for forestry but would contribute to biodiversity, water management, and stabilising steep slopes to reduce the risk of landslip. It is argued that the landslips that frequently block the Rest and be Thankful road would be much reduced, perhaps eliminated, if the slopes above the road were wooded instead of, as present, being denuded by grazing sheep and deer.

Unlocking the latent value in Scotland's land

In 1996, John Arlidge wrote in The Independent[9] that "half of Scotland is owned by just 500 people, few of whom are actually Scots." According to recent research by Green MSP Andy Wightman, 750,000 acres of Scotland, or about 4% of its total land area, is owned in tax havens[10]. The Scottish Government is embarking on a new phase of land reform[11]. The approach is very gradual, with the bolder recommendations of recent studies set aside for the moment.

When we started work on this chapter, we thought that land ownership reform was the key. As we developed our understanding, we realised that while it's part of the puzzle, it's not the whole answer. Indeed, it may not even be a critical factor in our vision. What really matters is, first, to unlock the value in the land by improving the way it's used and managed; and, second, once the value is unlocked, to keep most of that extra value within the Scottish economy, in the form of jobs and investment, rather than all being siphoned off overseas.

So what do we mean here by 'value'? It is not just economic value, though that's obviously key to the 'wealthy' part of our vision. It is also social and environmental value, which are key to improving 'health' and proving 'wisdom.' More jobs, healthier communities, more productive and biodiverse landscape. Not just slicing the cake differently, but making a larger cake – and ensuring that the whole country benefits.

Two things, we can be sure, won't make the cake bigger.

One is splitting the land up into small-holdings and abandoning large scale commercial forestry and agriculture. No one is seriously suggesting the latter; but landowners hold up the spectre of Zimbabwe (where the white farmers were dispossessed, their land distributed to 'veterans,' and food production collapsed, crashing the whole economy) as a dire warning every time the topic is mentioned. The extreme positions, both on the Green and on the landowning side of the debate, are straw man arguments that wouldn't happen in reality; but they do show the strength of feeling that the topic generates.

The other thing that won't make the cake bigger is carrying on as we are. Many highland estates are bought as status symbols and run at a loss. Overgrazing by sheep, red and roe deer, and the regular heather-burning on grouse moors prevent natural woodland regeneration over large tracts of land – which are of little use for forestry or agriculture, but are eminently suitable for "rewilding" to improve biodiversity and carbon capture. Much of our commercial forestry is in plots that are too small for best management practices to be economical. A lot of tree planting (and indeed most agriculture and forestry on marginal land) is driven by subsidy rather than value-generation. Significant parts of our landscape could almost be described as subsidy farms. On our better land, farming practices are productive but create relatively few jobs, and are extractive rather than regenerative – chemical fertilisers are essential to preserve soil productivity, and farming is one of Scotland's biggest sources of greenhouse gas emissions (see next chapter). The economics of farming, with producer prices driven down by supermarkets' buying power and a lot of farm income dependent on the vagaries of subsidy regimes as well as weather, provide no incentive to farmers to explore different approaches. Even if they did, it would be a brave farmer who adopted new, unfamiliar and unproven techniques that required a wholesale change in management approach, and whose financial returns were uncertain. (Though, to be fair, there are some brave farmers out there.)

We immersed ourselves in the argument and listened carefully to both sides – the more responsible among the rewilding and reforesting community, as well as estate and farm owners. We learned that, contrary to popular belief, rewilding isn't about replacing people with wilderness – instead, it's about improving the environment in harmony with thriving rural communities. And to understand what's possible and get an idea of international best practice, we also looked at successful and productive forestry in other countries.

Our key realisation was that the land ownership issue, while certainly part of the puzzle, is only about the 'how' and the 'who,' and not about the 'what.' So to a large extent it's a distraction from our key purpose here. What really matters is improving land use and land management, to create more value within the Scottish economy – financial, societal and environmental. A lot can be done within the current land ownership regime in terms of imposing best practice by example, by regulation, and by appropriate tax structure. Forestry and farming concessions can be granted to operators and communities on long leases without changing the ownership. If forestry and farming focus on maximising productivity per hectare rather than per employee, more jobs will be created, and more land will remain available for leisure and biodiversity purposes.

The additional investment required is unlikely to come from existing landowners, unless we can encourage them to take a much longer perspective and invest some of their wealth in a way that they don't currently. If only they had invested in forestry 40 years ago, their land would be worth a lot more now. We'll discuss various options in later chapters, all of which might have a part to play.

What could we do about it?

So far, we have lacked the collective will to tackle the barriers and accelerate the programme. Funding is modest, limited to moderate tweaks to existing subsidy regimes. Fourteen million trees were planted in 2018. If every able person in Scotland were to plant a hundred trees each, we could have at least 200 million new trees, making the progress thus far appear not so ambitious. One author planted 30 trees in a weekend with a spade costing £28, and £300 for the trees. Professional tree planters can plant over a thousand in a day. We could and should do more.

Plant more trees

One way forward would be a massive planting programme: past Forestry Commission efforts on steroids. We advocate aiming to triple this sector, which already produces close to £1 billion in GVA for the economy and maintains 25,000 direct jobs. To be clear, most of these jobs are in other parts of the value chain beyond forestry itself. There aren't many jobs in planting, managing and felling trees, and there will be fewer in future as modern automation takes more of the drudgery out of forestry. Sweden aspires to massively automate forest operations. A tripling of the jobs would require a much more substantial shift to Scotland becoming a wood-based economy as a whole.

This approach has four big advantages for Scotland.

Firstly, it fits neatly into the urgent timeframe of the environmental programme. Recent research by the Swiss University ETH Zurich concluded, "Restoration of trees remains among the most effective strategies for climate change mitigation[12]."

Furthermore, an upfront investment of a few billion pounds would provide a long-term economic stimulus to replace the expected decline in fossil fuel jobs. It has the rare advantage of spreading investment and jobs throughout the whole of Scotland, particularly in deprived areas reliant on subsistence farming. It could be one of the pillars of a much-needed Keynesian stimulus for the overall economy as an antidote to the economic devastation of Covid-19.

In addition, if managed carefully and with an eye on biodiversity, the restoration of Scotland's forests can produce trees suitable to Scotland's future timber needs. Scotland currently imports some grades of wood for building and construction. These could be grown here instead. As we shall discuss in a future chapter, a planned replanting would fit in with a desire to use more wood in smarter infrastructure and house building.

Finally, this forestry boom could help pay for the restoration of other parts of Scotland's neglected land – for example, the tax money could be used to reinstate our degenerated peat bogs. Deep peat bogs cover over ten percent of Scotland's land, and are crucial as carbon sinks; but many are degraded and need repairing. Yet this spending on peat bogs is problematic to some, because it provides no short-term financial return, only a longer term and more diffuse environmental benefit.

Seeing the wood for the trees

Let's not over-invest in last century's methods. Our assumptions and experience pre-programme us to assume the only way to address such issues is to do things "to" the environment, engineer fashion, at an industrial scale. But do we need to plant trees at all? There is another way, albeit much slower – let nature do the work for us. Trees regenerate naturally if protected from overgrazing by sheep and deer. Trial areas in the Highlands have been fenced in to allow plants to thrive without destructive interference by grazing animals. Within two decades they became virtually impenetrable, thick with regenerating trees, and a wide variety of succulent plants. This isn't the case everywhere. Nature needs human help unless there are suitable 'parent' trees, fertile soil, and protection from over-grazing. The snag with this approach is that the chance of creating a commercial industry with the right trees, jobs, and economic stimulus is much smaller.

This isn't an either-or choice, it's yes-and. We'd like to see woodland covering 50-70% of Scotland. A lot of it would be commercial forestry. The rest would be naturally rewilded, or human-assisted as necessary, both on marginal land not suitable for commercial timber (e.g. boggy, peaty, rocky, too high, inaccessible, subject to wind-throw hazard…), and in nooks and crannies on farmland and other open ground.

Save a tree, eat a deer?

Protection for young trees doesn't even need to involve expensive infrastructure such as deer fences, not always anyway. In a recent submission to the Scottish Parliament's Rural Affairs, Climate Change and Environment Committee[13], Reforesting Scotland pointed out that "heavy culling at an estate level is sufficient to reduce deer numbers to levels where tree regeneration can take place over large areas and without fencing." This has been demonstrated in Glen Feshie, Mar Lodge, Creag Meagaidh and Abernethy in the Central Highlands, and Carrifran in the Southern Uplands. And because there is no fencing to keep them out, the deer can shelter in the woodlands in bad weather, so the surviving population becomes healthier. Counter-intuitively, it also seems that sporting revenues are not significantly affected. Better quality makes up for smaller quantities.

"Save a tree, eat a deer" is a harsh reality that is the subject of much controversy[14]. Approximately 100,000 red deer are shot in sporting estates each year. This is just enough to keep the population stable, but the truth is there are too many deer. The red deer population needs to be reduced by around two-thirds to allow natural woodland regeneration.

When red deer move in herds on the open hillside, they are clear for all to see. Roe deer are woodland animals – much less noticeable than red deer but present in similar numbers, and equally problematic for woodland regeneration. Roe deer had to be excluded from the Carrifran wildwood to allow regeneration. Numbers are on the rise throughout Scotland. A friend of the authors reports that on a nearby estate in East Lothian, the keepers used to shoot one or two roe deer a year; while now they shoot about 60. And roe deer are much more difficult to shoot than red deer.

Reforesting Scotland's "A Forest for the Future" report[15] provides a great road map of what's possible and desirable, albeit we'd like to be even more ambitious. Common Weal's "Back to Life" report[16] highlights the potential economic benefits. Ruth Tingay's and Andy Wightman's "Revive" report[17] illustrates some of the costs and lost opportunities of the current set-up. To quote Amie Dow of the John Muir Trust, proudly showing the regenerating natural woodland in Knoydart to a visitor, "This is what the whole of the Highlands should look like: big, open glades, alongside areas of dense forest[18]."

How many trees are we talking about? Commercial woodland typically has 2,500 trees per hectare after five years of growth, thinned down over time to perhaps 500 by the time the trees are mature. A hectare is an area of 10,000 square metres, the size of a typical football stadium. So, if you can imagine Hampden covered with 2,500 young trees, or 500 mature ones, you're imagining one hectare of woodland. We're talking about up to an extra two million hectares of commercial forestry, and 1-2 million more of naturally regenerated wood and scrub land. Between planting and natural regeneration, we're talking about something in excess of five billion new trees, above and beyond what's required to keep renewing the current forestry estate.

Now, we don't want to blanket Scotland and block the views with a boring expanse of conifers – "pines in lines" – although to kick start any major commercial planting some of this will be required. Planting trees close together encourages them to grow straight; after thinning, the healthiest should be allowed to grow to yield a cubic metre of timber each. A mix of tree types is beneficial. High up on the mountains, where trees won't grow to full height, the new 'woodland' will be scrub rather than proper trees.

Does engineered wood change the rules of the game?

Traditionally, if you wanted a large piece of wood for construction, you needed to cut it from the trunk of a large tree. Modern technologies such as Glulam (glue laminated timber), CLT (cross laminated timber) and LVL (laminated veneer lumber) produce large custom-shaped wooden structural components, fire resistant and as strong as steel, by gluing together good quality but smaller pieces of wood. Typical "lamstock" (feedstock for Glulam manufacture) is 5-30 cm wide, by 2-8 metres long[19]. This is a well-established technology, using a high degree of automation. We'll come back to this later. For now, we note that engineered wood is a viable structural material for large buildings; and because lamstock is smaller than structural timbers, it may be possible to use younger trees, giving faster investment returns.

Transform farming

As well as deer, overgrazing by sheep – Fraser Darling's "woolly locusts" – is another problem. Recent estimates for sheep numbers in Scotland are in the region of 2.5 million, and our sheep farming model depends on subsidies. It's also time to reform agriculture.

Agriculture accounts for 23% of humanity's global carbon footprint[20]. In 2017[21], Scotland's agriculture and agriculture-related land-use emissions were indeed about 23% of our net emissions. These emissions were pretty much balanced by the carbon absorbed by our forests. That sounds good. But, to put it another way, all the climate benefits of our trees were wiped out by emissions from our farms.

However, zero-emission 'regenerative' agriculture methods are now well understood, and Scottish farming thus has the potential to become a carbon restoring rather than carbon emitting enterprise. Some of the best farms may have already begun their transition to being carbon-restoring, but, as we've just seen, when considering Scotland as a whole agriculture's emissions remain only at around the world average. Additional benefits of regenerative agriculture include increased soil carbon content, increased biodiversity, reduction or elimination of artificial fertiliser use, less run-off of soil and chemicals, and reduced flood risk because the ground absorbs more water. A good example of these new techniques is seen at Balbirnie Mains Farm in Fife with a new generation of innovative farmers and farming.

Forestry and agriculture are usually seen as an "either-or" choice. It's widely assumed that we can do one or the other on any piece of land, but not both. In spite of this conviction, though, techniques such as agroforestry – one of the widely discussed approaches to regenerative agriculture – are specifically designed to offer the best of both worlds. According to the UN's Food and Agriculture Organisation (FAO)[22], "agroforestry represents an interesting option especially in those areas where the need for landscape restoration is associated with the need for increased food and fuel production." There are various flavours of agroforestry, ranging from simple shelter belts, to fully integrated cropping of both forest and food products. Project Drawdown[23] asserts that "multistrata agroforestry can be integrated into some existing agricultural systems; others can be converted or restored to it… Average sequestration rate … is strong, as is financial return[24]."

Planting densities for agroforestry are lower than for dedicated forestry. Grants are available in Scotland for agroforestry planting at 200 trees per hectare, as opposed to 2,000+ for 'forestry'. The lower planting density permissible for agroforestry is anathema to serious foresters, because the resulting trees are less regimented, yielding poorer quality timber that is much less useful for wood product industries.

One interesting form of agroforestry is silvopasture[25], where animals graze in woodland instead of open pastures. The animals benefit from the trees' shelter, they emit less methane, and more carbon is sequestered in – trampled into - the ground.

Why would we dismiss an approach that gives a positive return on investment, and helps to solve the climate crisis, and to repair the damage of hundreds of years of neglect and misuse of the land?

Well, one major damper is that regenerative agriculture is likely to be more labour intensive than industrial farming techniques, a problem for a country with high labour costs such as Scotland. This could also potentially lead to higher food prices, unless the increased cost is offset by carbon credits and savings elsewhere in the economy. For example, since woodland reduces the costs of flooding and flood prevention, some of those savings could be paid out to farmers who switch to agroforestry.

Another issue, as the FAO points out, is that "because agroforestry integrates multiple natural components and is at the crossroads of tradition and modernity, it necessarily brings together people from diverse fields of knowledge: agronomists, animal care specialists, landscape planners, foresters, economists, soil analysts and many more. This diversity of disciplines is certainly a strength, but its complexity also represents a challenge, notably in terms of coordination and communication." Scotland has all these business, financial, social, and ecological skills, and abundant local knowledge. If anyone can do this, surely Scotland can?

Another area where Scotland would seem to have the skills but not, as yet, the ambition, is the field known as 'Agtech,' or 'Agricultural technology.' Israel and the Netherlands are current leaders, the latter being involved in 'the world's largest indoor farm,' now being built in Abu Dhabi[26]. This will showcase techniques to increase food production in extreme climates, while reducing environmental impact. Other areas of interest include sensing crop condition, precise fertilisation and irrigation, disease tracking, maximising yields, reducing cost and environmental impact, and tracing physical product through the supply chain. The latter improves efficiency and reduces waste, and certifies place of origin and integrity of process, for example to confirm a product's organic or vegan or low-carbon credentials. Agtech is emerging as a hot topic for investors[27].

Making these changes will take time – a lot of time. Most farmers are deeply sceptical about any new method, with some reason. Margins for food producers are very tight, due to the buying power of supermarket chains; so any change that disrupts their production or increases their costs even for a short period is viewed with extreme suspicion. Few farmers will adopt new methods until they have seen the benefit in their own neighbourhood with their own eyes. The shift won't happen without a big investment in demonstrator farms, to showcase the new methods and educate people in their use.

Economic value of different land use options

The opportunities are substantial if we can shift Scotland's land use towards more productive and higher value-added activities, such as forestry and regenerative agriculture. Common Weal's Policy Paper "Back to Life" provides the following estimates, compiled by analysing data from a number of sources[28]. None of this analysis, as far as we know, includes the potential value of carbon credits, if and when there is a realistic worldwide carbon price.

Deer stalking is missing from the list, but it's hard to imagine it creates much more value than grouse shooting.

Land Use	Annual GVA £ per Hectare	Hectares to create one job
Horticulture	12,412	3
Housing	11,950	7
Solar	10,952	no estimate
Forestry	900	42 (*)
Agriculture	509	183
Grouse shooting	30	330

(*) The various 'hectares per job' figures may not be directly comparable, as they are necessarily compiled using a disparate range of data sources. The forestry figure is based on the entire extended value chain of direct and indirect jobs, which is not the case for all the others.

The most disconcerting conclusion from these figures is how unproductive grouse shooting is. The value added per hectare is negligible compared with any other land use, and the employment created – often claimed to be 'vital for the survival of local communities' – is minimal, mostly seasonal, and (based on these numbers) appears to pay less than minimum wage[29]. Surely there are better uses for this 'empty quarter' (or at least empty eighth) of our country?

Reach for the moon!

Our 18-60 Vision

We advocate an ambitious programme to jump from 18 to 60% woodland cover over the period 2018 to 2060 – hence the name '18-60'; and a switch over the same period from traditional, semi-subsidised farming to modern regenerative agriculture.

This might seem as ambitious as putting a Man on the Moon. So be it! It's time we found positive national "Moon-shot" projects that are tangible and productive for society as a whole. The programme is multifaceted, requiring a coordination from both central Government and local communities. It involves contentious actions to overcome or resolve minority interests. Our plea therefore – set a new, much accelerated programme, lifting the targets from 21% woodland cover in 2032 to 50% by 2050 and 60% by 2060. This is one of the biggest economic stimuli that Scotland can realise in the foreseeable future. The vision has five components.

1. **Triple the commercial forestry and wood product industries**, to contribute 3% to GDP and replace most of the UK timber imports with home-grown timber products. This means up to 2 million additional hectares of high-productivity forests managed to the best international standards, and state of the art wood processing plants – sawmills, glulam plant – established close to the main woodland areas and with good access for export to Scottish markets and further afield.

2. **Promote wooden housing** to create a home market for this new industry. This would address both the need for long-term carbon sequestration in harvested timber and the need for housing. *'Burning a tree keeps you warm for a week. Insulating your house with the wood will keep you warm for a lifetime.'* We want to see a massive public-sector-led programme to build new low-cost good-quality modular social housing to zero carbon "Passiv Haus" standards or equivalent[30]. A large programme of zero carbon modular wooden housing, using Scottish timber only, would stimulate demand for home-grown timber and replanting in a similar fashion to Sweden and Finland.

3. **Rewild marginal land to create 'conservation woodland':** rewild most of our current rough grazing, deer forests and grouse moors, creating up to 2 million hectares of 'conservation woodland' by 2070, with an end to the practice of regular 'muirburn' on grouse moors, and with grazing pressure from sheep and red and roe deer reduced to sustainable levels.

4. **Transform agriculture from extractive to regenerative:** a strategic national shift of farming over the next generation from extractive to regenerative agriculture – spearheaded by regenerative farming and Agtech research/demonstrator projects across the country to learn and disseminate the new methods.

5. **Enhance provision for leisure land use** with appropriate infrastructure and facilities, so that more people can enjoy the countryside more often while reducing pressure on the environment and rural communities.

The three core arguments for the 18-60 vision

There are three fundamental arguments for this very high level of ambition.

First of all, the environmental argument. The increase in commercial and conservation woodland, and the switch to regenerative agriculture, offer many environmental advantages including: an increase in biodiversity and soil health; a reduction in fertiliser and biocide use; an increase in carbon drawdown and sequestration; an improvement in water management, reducing landslips affecting road and rail links; the provision of better winter cover for deer and other animals, and an increased scope for agroforestry; and the replacement of carbon-intensive imported steel and concrete with carbon-storing home-grown and home-manufactured engineered timber.

Secondly, the social argument. The 18-60 vision should create over 20,000 new good quality and steady jobs throughout rural Scotland, restore the health of local communities, and encourage investment in transport and social infrastructure across the country.

And, thirdly the economic argument. Economic benefits of the 18-60 vision include: import substitution for much of the UK's current wood product imports (apart from wood pellets and some specialised species and products); the adoption of 21st century practices for factory-built custom modular homes using the new high-tech wood building materials and techniques; an improvement in land utilisation, forest productivity and land value thanks to the introduction of modern world-class high-yield forest management techniques; and an acceleration of the economic return due to improved growth rates, tree size and timber quality. Some sources[31] also claim that large Glulam structural components can be made using smaller and younger trees than the 50-70-year specimens required to make solid-sawn structural timbers, further accelerating the economic return.

There are big challenges

Increasing woodland cover from 18 to 60% is a big challenge. And doing it in a way that delivers all the intended benefits is a bigger challenge still. Here are our top ten issues that will need serious attention.

1. Achieving the right balance of rewilding, commercial forestry, agro-forestry, active interventions for biodiversity and water catchment management/landslip mitigation.

2. Introducing effective regenerative agriculture with methods suitable for Scotland: research/demonstration farms, with a major re-education programme, and a new regime for agriculture and environmental payments.

3. Bringing all estates up to the level of the highest performers, in terms of social, environmental and economic benefits (using comprehensive holistic standards for estate and benefits management, and an effective incentivisation/enforcement regime; and almost certainly, consolidating small penny packets into larger areas of concentrated woodland planted on suitable ground).

4. Establishing and growing high tech, top quality wood, housing, and paper businesses.

5. Reassessing foreign land ownership, its impact on land and housing practices, sustainable development, affordable housing for moderately paid professionals and minimum wage local workers.

6. Reassessing taxation and ownership rights of underutilised and degraded land: carbon tax, land value tax or annual ground rent, compulsory purchase, equitable treatment of windfall gains from rezoning – we hear a wide range of views from across the political spectrum, we're not taking sides.

7. Ensuring continued leisure access and path systems, and encouraging healthy exercise including long distance cycling and walking. Discourage excessive driving and vehicle use.

8. Building up and strengthening local communities, including delegating responsibility to communities for conservation management where the relevant competence exists.

9. Funding the entire enterprise. Some of the required money could be generated by the Forestry Commission selling long term leases to manage, improve, harvest, and renew its current estate (this raises the cash without taking the contentious step of selling off publicly owned land, possibly to foreign investors); more by offering attractive long-term propositions to pension funds and sovereign wealth funds looking for sustainable post-oil revenue streams.

10. Avoiding over bureaucratisation and excessive centralised management in pursuit of 1-9!

An example of what it might mean[32]

In addition to the current 900,000 hectares of conifers, a further 2 million hectares of commercial forest could be planted. If done over a period of 20 years that implies a planting rate of 100,000 hectares, or 200 million trees, per year. That's a major challenge. We believe the most the UK has ever planted is 30-40 thousand additional hectares a year, for a year or two in the 80s. At that rate, planting another two million hectares would take 60 years. Even at 50,000 hectares/yr it would take until 2060 to complete the additional planting – and of course this is on top of the rotational replanting of existing forestry. A challenge indeed.

At the end of this, the total commercial estate would be, say, 3 million hectares and should have a production rate of 7m3/ha/year. This should be achievable, compared with the current 5.7 m3/ha/year, with better land and forest management. Once the additional commercial forests are fully established, production of around 20 million m^3 can be achieved. The extra production is similar to current UK imports of sawn timber and wood-based panels, worth at least £4bn per year. It may take 50 years to reach this amount, depending on the speed of establishing new forest, but with thinning starting to occur 15-20 years after planting, increased production will be evident. With replanting and good management this production rate can be sustained indefinitely.

Commercial forestry is more efficient if managed in large lots. The minimum viable forest is 400 ha for modern yield-enhancement techniques such as effective thinning. Yet

40ha is a typical woodland plot at the moment. We should only plant trees on land where they'll grow well – leave the wet boggy bits, and the inaccessible bits, and the peaty bits, and the areas subject to high wind-throw hazard, to be part of the rewilding conservation woodland.

Another 2 million hectares could be rewilded or converted to managed conservation woodland over the 50 years if we were to stop muirburn and bring grazing pressure down to sustainable levels to allow natural regeneration of woodland in marginal land. That's a rate of 40,000 ha/yr. The end of sheep subsidies with Brexit will help. It would also be necessary to increase red deer cull quotas and intensify control of roe deer. A highly controversial proposal – more acceptable perhaps if sheep numbers are reduced – is the reintroduction of the lynx, an approach favoured by part of the rewilding fraternity. There wouldn't need to be that many, because experience from Yellowstone shows that introducing even a small number of apex predators (wolves in that case) reduces grazing pressure over wide areas by keeping grazing animals moving. We're agnostic on this, but would point out that reintroducing lynx could well be the best way to control roe deer numbers and grazing pressure, as roe deer are difficult to find and shoot in their native woodland habitat.

Because we propose only to plant commercial trees where they will grow well, there will be more glades and gaps than in current commercial forests, even in the first crop rotation. As thinning and replanting continues over multiple rotations, any impression of 'pines in lines' will be significantly mitigated from 2070 when most of the land will be in its second rotation.

As far as the farming transformation is concerned, regenerative farming and Agtech demonstrator projects could be launched in the next five years, to pave the way for widespread commercial adoption by 2040. These onshore farming demonstrator projects could go hand in hand with similar experiments in marine-based agriculture which we mention in chapter 6. A stewardship of both land and sea that would benefit Scotland.

It's not a zero-sum game

Too many people see the land use arguments as either-or choices: field sports or rewilding; farming or forestry; carbon sequestration or economically useful activity; nature or people.

A 'win-lose' or 'zero-sum' situation. We believe that there is so much underutilised land that could be stewarded more effectively that a win-win is entirely possible. Not an either-or but a 'yes-and'. Not that everyone gets everything they want, but most people can win something. It's about restoring a deeply damaged ecosystem to a thriving, healthy, resilient state that will support people and nature, forestry and farming, jobs and leisure, carbon sequestration and biodiversity and adaptation to climate change – healthy and resilient communities in a healthy and resilient landscape.

A healthy biodiverse landscape is good for nature and good for communities. Restored woodland and wetlands absorb more rain and have less and slower run-off than over-fertilised fields or barren moorland. This means that downstream communities are less at risk of flash flooding, and the water is better quality. It also supports a greater number and variety of plants, animals, insects, fungi and microbes. In stark economic terms, a healthy ecosystem means we spend less on flood defences and insurance claims.

At the country level we can make the cake bigger, by putting each parcel of land throughout Scotland to its most appropriate use. Avoid trying to cultivate and drain marginal land – set it aside for rewilding and renewable energy and outdoor sports. Use well drained fertile land for forestry or farming, or innovative agroforestry. Concentrate commercial forestry close to processing plants to get the economies of scale. Increase the quality and yield of commercial forestry to release more land for other purposes. Do more of the value-added processing of timber, and of food, near to where it's grown to put more wealth and jobs into rural communities. Adapt field sports to styles that take full advantage of the more varied landscape.

Fundamentally, it's about having the wisdom to put the right tree in the right place for the right reason. Nevertheless, some Scots will face radical changes. Traditional farmers and some landowners will find the adjustment hard.

An Estate Owners' Conversation in 2040

Mary sat in front of her wood-burning stove, flicking through the large photo album left to her by her parents. They had passed away ten years ago to the day. The wind was howling outside, and the torrential rain was pounding against the glass windows of their old estate house in the heart of the Scottish Highlands.

Her parents had experienced a disappointing end to their lives. The various land reform acts and changes in incentives had caused them to sell their 10,000-acre purple-heathered estate and farm holding. They were left with 40 acres of land round the house, and a 250-acre livestock farm run by a single manager living in the nearby old estate cottage. They never really got over the massive changes forced on them as they entered their 80s. Mary was saddened, but she had seen it coming.

What had upset her most were the lost fireside chats with the fascinating people who came from all around the globe. Gone were some of the wonderful characters who used to enrich the dining and living rooms throughout the year. Neither the short-let tourists, nor the users of the new modest forest huts that had spread like wildfire, now visited the estate house.

Just as she was beginning to spiral down into nostalgic gloom, her younger brother based in Ullapool called. He was the manager of a new biodiverse forested estate, part of the 40-year programme, some planted, some natural, to grow three billion trees in Scotland, initially triggered in 2024. The first part of that programme had gone badly in the first few years from the lack of promised funding and slower natural growth than the impatient policy makers had predicted. The other snag had been disputes between competing campaigns to allocate more resources to peat bog restoration, with some traditional agriculturalists wanting more of the land for livestock, and the well-funded Biodiversity Society of Scotland, run from Regents Terrace in Edinburgh, trying to slow everything down.

However, now that the Norwegian Sovereign Wealth Fund had agreed to inject £2 billion into Scottish forest restoration as part of their own diversification out of fossil fuels, the programme was accelerating nicely.

"Blowing a gale here. How's the weather on your side?" Richard asked.

"Wind just picked up. The rain is now torrential," Mary replied.

"I am really calling to find out if there was any news," explained Richard.

"What about?" asked Mary.

"From our lawyers on the appeal against the farm manager's rights to purchase the farm. I am still annoyed that he suddenly became interested, now that our neighbours are succeeding with their small agroforestry initiative," replied Richard.

"No news yet."

"Lawyers – slow as usual. Never mind, I'll call again next week," he said.

Mary returned to her earlier mood and changed the subject. "You know Richard, what I miss the most?"

"No. Tell me."

"Most of all, I miss the company and the life about the house. The house guests used to eat a hearty English breakfast over the kitchen table, exchanging their tales. Great fun…

"But you know, the other thing that bugs me is walking up to the Duke of Gordon Monument. My favourite view of the Spey Valley is gone. Best view in the valley. From Kingussie in the south and beyond Aviemore in the north. Trees blocking the view now!"

"Next thing, you'll be saying it's all my fault!" interjected Richard. "At least we're creating new jobs. Locals are happy."

He added, "Somebody said recently we had passed the one billion tree mark. Timber getting close to one and half per cent of the economy. The new village communities established in Sutherland around forestry expansion were featured on TV last night. Did you see it?"

Mary speculated, "Maybe we should have persuaded our parents to have bitten the bullet. Borrowed to pay for a reinvestment in commercial forestry and for the extra land tax. Could have invested in even more tourism in the forests when the sheep farming subsidies were phased out. The McDougalls in our neighbouring estate have had a real go at creating new businesses to pay for their debt. They've done well. Well beyond glamping and tourist huts and forest walks. All three of us could still be working here together if we had done the same."

Richard responded. "Yes, you're probably right. It was a real dilemma. Hard to see a way through at the time. Maybe, if we had taken the forty-year view, borrowed at the low interest rates, post Covid – remember those days – we might all be together still? We could have held on to the estate, planted a few million trees. Converted ourselves into a forestry family like some of our Swedish friends. That new construction wood business – Glulam – could have been our future. Glulam from the valley! Might have retired by now. Sold it to some rich Norwegian or Swedish forester. All living in Bermuda rather than Ullapool or Russia?"

"Oh well," commented Mary. "Easy to say in hindsight, our parents were too old by then. To be honest, it was us that were short-sighted. Mind you, it would have been a tough transition."

Richard changed the subject. "How's Sheonagh getting on with her move to Northern Russia anyway? Not my idea of fun." Sheonagh was Mary's only daughter.

"Just spoke to her yesterday as it happens," Mary replied. "She's loving it. Donald is adjusting having found a job there himself. Mind you, she's finding it difficult to learn Russian and deal with the male culture. Not an easy language and definitely not easy for a woman in business. The kids seem to be doing OK. At least Milo has found the transition from Gaelic to Russian much easier. Quite a Scots community over there. The new port construction project run by that Glasgow firm, McNeil and McNeil, seems to be doing very well. You know DP World, who own them, don't you? The world's largest port operator. Based in Dubai. They won a large part of Putin's so-called Ice Silk Route. Tricky move for McNeil to set up a base in Russia. Still can't pronounce the new city she's based in."

"Glad for Sheonagh, Scotland getting its act together to win some business up there," commented Richard.

He continued, "Glasgow and Orkney have really done well. I hear that Orkney and Inverness have had significant immigration for the first time in a while. Even our nephew James in London is thinking of moving back to Glasgow for the financing of the expansion of Scapa Flow."

Mary added her own observation, "Strange really. Our dad used to say we should look to our future in America. He said it was time to leave. Yet here we are, creeping further North.

Who would have thought that 30 years ago? Reagan must be turning in his grave at Russia having a new lease of life from the Arctic boom!"

"Aye," responded Richard, "Remember the USA falling out with Russia again… over the Arctic!" He added, "But the forestry boom has been a godsend for Xana and me. Managing a team of forty new recruits at the moment. Five thousand new jobs on the west coast alone… Anyway, must go… the wild west is tiring me out. Speak to you next week."

"Good to hear things are going well," concluded Mary, as she sank back into her chair. She flicked through the final pages of the photo album and enjoyed the last warmth from the embers of the dying fire.

"The best time to plant a tree was 20 years ago. The next best time is now."

Chinese Proverb

References for Chapter 3

[1] Food & Agriculture Organisation Data, % of Land Use, 2017

[2] https://www.nature.scot/professional-advice/land-and-sea-management/managing-land/forests-and-woodlands/history-scotlands-woodlands

[3] On 1st April 2019, Forestry Commission Scotland became Scottish Forestry, an executive agency of the Scottish Government (grants, research). Forest Enterprise became Forestry and Land Scotland (forest managers).

[4] https://forestry.gov.scot/images/corporate/pdf/economic-contribution-forestry-2015.pdf

[5] https://www.gov.scot/publications/scotlands-forestry-strategy-20192029/pages/4/

[6] Royal Swedish Academy of Agriculture & Forestry, Forests and Forestry in Sweden, August 2015

[7] Our own estimate based on direct and indirect employment levels for current level of forestry.

[8] Scottish Forest and Timber Technologies, Roots for Future Growth (2011), p. 31
http://www.forestryscotland.com/media/101263/rffg%20lower%20res%20web%20version%202.pdf

[9] https://www.independent.co.uk/news/uk/home-news/who-owns-scotland-1320933.html

[10] http://www.andywightman.com/archives/category/who-owns-scotland

[11] https://www.gov.scot/policies/land-reform/; Andy Wightman's essay in "Scotland the Brave?" Luath Press, July 2019

[12] The global tree restoration potential, Science, 5 July 2019, Bastin JF, Finegold Y, Garcia C, Mollicone D, Rezende M, Routh D, Zohner CM, Crowther TW

[13] http://www.reforestingscotland.org/what-we-do/influencing-policy/the-impact-and-management-of-deer-in-scotland/

[14] https://www.theguardian.com/news/2018/feb/20/deer-cull-dilemma-scottish-highlands

[15] https://www.reforestingscotland.org/a-forest-for-the-future/

[16] https://commonweal.scot/sites/default/files/2019-02/Back%20to%20Life.pdf

[17] http://revive.scot/wp-content/uploads/ReviveReport.pdf

[18] Amie Dow, Knoydart ranger, John Muir Trust Journal 67 – Autumn 2019.

[19] https://www.kalesnikoff.com/products/lumber

[20] Berners-Lee, Mike, "There's No Planet B," Cambridge University Press, Cambridge, 2019, estimates 23% for Agriculture (p22). UN Global Sustainable Development report 2019 estimates 24% for "Agriculture, forestry and other land use". Other sectors' contributions are energy 34%, industry 21%, transport 14%, building 6%. (p58)

[21] https://www.gov.scot/publications/scottish-greenhouse-gas-emissions-2017/pages/3/

[22] http://www.fao.org/forestry/agroforestry/en/, accessed 15th August 2019

[23] www.drawdown.org, also Paul Hawken, Drawdown: The Most Comprehensive Plan Ever Proposed to Reverse Global Warming, Penguin Books 22 Feb 2018

[24] https://www.drawdown.org/solutions/food/multistrata-agroforestry

[25] https://www.drawdown.org/solutions/food/silvopasture

[26] https://www.thenational.ae/uae/environment/abu-dhabi-to-build-world-s-biggest-indoor-farm-1.1082447

[27] https://home.kpmg/au/en/home/insights/2018/08/venture-capital-investment-agtech.html

[28] Back to Life, Common Weal, 10/12/2018 Thanks to Craig Dalzell for confirming his sources, and for Robin MacAlpine for permission to use.

[29] Though it's difficult to get a good figure for full time equivalent jobs in grouse shooting because most of the employment is seasonal and casual.

[30] Common Weal is now promoting this too – Craig Dalzell, *Good houses for all: how Scotland can build unlimited homes - without subsidy*, Common Weal Policy Paper, May 2020

[31] APA – The Engineered Wood Association, 2008, Glulam Product Guide https://law.resource.org/pub/us/code/bsc.ca.gov/sibr/org.apawood.X440.pdf

[32] We are grateful to David Balfour for his comprehensive advice how the vision might be realised in practice.

Chapter 4

Renewing Renewables – the Power of Scotland

"The economy is a wholly owned subsidiary of the environment, not the reverse." Herman E. Dal

"Earth provides enough to satisfy every man's needs, but not every man's greed." Mahatma Gandhi

"The stone age did not end because the world ran out of stone. And the oil age will not end because we run out of oil." Ahmed Zaki Yamani, Minister of Oil for Saudi Arabia

Scotland and the rest of the UK missed an opportunity. We should have, like Denmark, invested strategically in renewable energy, recognising it as a long-term trend. We can recover some of that lost ground in the next generation of renewable technologies. And equally, we can become a major net exporter of renewable energy. But if we want to take advantage of this potential, business as usual won't hack it. We need a national policy and strategic investment to create wealth and new employment – an ambitious large-scale programme, keeping much more of the added value in Scotland, with vision, leadership and substantial funding provided by 'the entrepreneurial state'.

"How fast to wean ourselves off the fossils" – a pre-Covid-19 view

Michael spotted his friend across the crowded ante room. "Damien," he bellowed, attracting disapproving glances. Shyness was not one of his character traits. "How about a coffee across the Mall at Café Nero?"

"Good idea. I really need a triple espresso after that grilling," Damien called back.

They were in the prestigious Prince Philip House in London, home of the Royal Academy of Engineering. The summer of 2019 was the northern hemisphere's hottest on record[1], and here in England, this was the hottest day of that year. The conference on the future of the UK oil and gas industry had just ended. Damien Black, the Chief Economist of Grampian Oil, was wilting – he had barely survived the final hostile question-and-answer panel session.

"See you there in a few minutes", said Michael, as he passed Damien on his way to the cloakroom.

* * *

The panel was an interesting mix of economists, environmentalists and scientists. The audience, sweltering in the poorly air-conditioned room, mainly comprised environmentalists and scientists, with a few oil executives. The industry mood was complacent. No-one had the faintest inkling of the pandemic chaos and price war that were to come the following year.

Damien started his controversial speech with the words "The Stone Age didn't end because we ran out of stone. It ended because we found better and easier materials."

"By analogy, it's nonsense to suggest that we'll run out of oil and gas any time soon, in the world, or even in British waters. There's plenty left, probably two to three hundred years' worth. Proven world oil reserves stand at 50 years[2]. Add in further discoveries, say 20 years, and another thirty for heavy oil and unconventional resources, then a much better estimate is

90 years economical supply worldwide with current technology. As everyone in the Industry knows, MIT[3] reckon that two thirds of the oil in known fields is still in the ground because the technology is not yet good enough.

"The Oil and Gas Authority (OGA) is now predicting that 11.9 billion barrels of oil will be extracted from the North Sea and west of Shetland by 2050. That's 49% up from the estimate of 8 billion barrels predicted four years ago, at the time of the Independence Referendum. That could be worth as much as a trillion pounds. The 2014 estimate of £150 billion was very pessimistic.

"I want to echo the thoughts of Lord Browne, former CEO of BP. As many of you know, he is now backed by a Russian billionaire, and they're investing heavily in increasing Mexican fossil fuel production for the next 30 years[4]. He maintains that in areas such as aviation, maritime and heavy commercial shipping, there are no viable substitutes for oil. Natural gas has a long life ahead, as it replaces coal in the power sector, and provides a reliable complement to the intermittency of renewables.

"As Browne himself suggested, and I quote, 'It is also premature to discount the ability of today's oil and gas companies to adapt. When I took over as CEO of BP in 1995, the industry invested almost nothing in renewable energy. Today, the 'supermajors' allocate more than $4 billion every year to low or zero-carbon energy. These giants have the resources to make large capital commitments, and in many cases, skills that can be adapted and redeployed to deliver energy solutions at the immense scale that is needed. If leaders can redirect their organisations toward a new lower-carbon purpose, and if they can successfully engage their staff, there is every reason to believe they can be active participants in, or even drivers of, the energy transition.' BP is getting a new boss in January. It will be interesting to see how enthusiastically he tackles this challenge." [As we now know, the answer is 'very'.]

The discussion degenerated into chaos when business analytics company IHS Markit presented their expectation that total demand for oil and gas would still rise by 30 percent between now and 2040. Consumption of renewable energy was expected to triple, but from a lower base: by 2040, it would account for just 6 percent of the energy mix, roughly the same as nuclear power today. IHS Markit were challenged by attendees who quoted BP showing a scenario where renewables could be as high as 15% by 2045. Some thought that was a gross underestimate, whereas others were extremely confident that this was much closer to reality. A confused debate ended with the admission that the situation is now changing so quickly that forecasts are no better than guesswork.

Damien put forward the case that much more investment was required to develop the obvious alternatives of wind, solar, and wave power. He also challenged politicians to stop obscuring the truth and stick to the facts. However nice it might be to place the blame of carbon emissions on aviation, the truth of the matter is that cars and vans account for 13% of the global carbon footprint, and over 50% of the European carbon footprint for transport in Europe. How can that compare to the mere 2% of global carbon emissions produced by aviation? He finished his intervention with a bombshell for those who had not heard him preach his radical carbon tax message before. "Politicians will need to prepare the ground for a further carbon tax on car fuel of somewhere between 50 pence and 6 pounds per gallon."

Michael, a professor at LSE, was the last panel member to speak. He provided a broad view of the history of the oil and gas industry and its impact on Scotland's economy.

"As you know, Oil and Gas fields were found in British waters in 1965. This was a fortunate time for Britain's economy – still struggling from the massive cost of the Second World War, the loss of wealth from the collapse of the Empire, and its failure to establish modern world-class manufacturing in shipbuilding, trains, cars, and bikes. Oil helped fuel a boom in the 1980s that made Thatcher look better than she really was at creating sustainable wealth for the UK. But a large part of this windfall, the 'Gift from God' as some Middle East countries describe it, was badly stewarded. Production was accelerated to pay back Britain's loans from the IMF in the 1970s – and to pay for the large-scale unemployment triggered by Thatcher's industrial policies in the 1980s.

"The IPPR think tank calculated that between 1980 and 1990 oil and gas generated £166 billion for the UK in taxes[5]. The Government used this windfall to spend above the UK's non-oil means. In my view, the decision not to set up a Sovereign Wealth Fund with this windfall was a fundamental strategic error – very poor stewarding of resources. Norway did set up a Sovereign Wealth Fund, and it's now worth well over $1 trillion.

"The Norwegians handled another strategic issue quite differently from us as well. Norway maintains a state-owned oil company, Equinor, for national strategic reasons. The older among us will remember the British National Oil Company (BNOC) – yes, we too had a state-owned oil company. I ask you, with the benefit of hindsight, do you think its privatisation was a wise choice?"

He paused and looked at the audience. They looked back, confused, not sure if they were expected to venture an opinion. As Michael continued, it became obvious the question had been rhetorical. "BNOC was established in Glasgow in 1975, but was privatised as Britoil and then swallowed up by BP. Was world leadership lost? Did lack of industrial policy allow major leaks in skills and resources? Even now, at this late stage, would Scotland be better served by establishing a National Oil Company to control the pace and focus of future development, and extract a greater share of the profits rather than let them leak out of the country? Nationalisation has its flaws, but what good has it done for the local economy to have international oil companies taking their profits abroad?"

He challenged the industry, but mainly politicians, to give a much clearer picture on how to cut the use of fossil fuels in the economy and criticised them for paying lip-service to the issue. He recalled the slogan of BP going 'Beyond Petroleum' and asked how much had the oil industry or its shareholders really invested in renewables?

* * *

Michael walked across the road, met Damien, and ordered a green tea, in contrast to his fellow speaker's much needed double expresso.

"So, Michael, what do you think of Sir Ian Wood's comments about oil at the last Scottish Independence referendum in 2014?"

"Well, it was obvious what he wanted to prove with his comments. A Unionist at heart. Of course, everyone, immediately after, thought he had it right, what with the oil price collapsing to a low of $27 per barrel WTI in 2015[6]. But that didn't last long, did it? Bounced back to what the economists thought would be the long-term price, more like $60-70 per barrel. Anyway, I agree with you; it's not a matter of running out of North Sea Oil. Plenty for at least another 90 years, some say longer. It's when we stop needing it because we have seriously invested in the alternative, and consumers have stopped using their gas-guzzling cars and lifestyles."

Damien interjected, "Yes, and as you said, the sad and crazy thing is Britain has no Sovereign Wealth Fund from the oil bonanza in the 1980s. I hadn't seen it quite so clearly before. That 'gift from God' is a great phrase! The discovery of oil fooled both Britain and future Thatcherites into believing we had a newly found source of economic wealth from adopting a free market economy, rather than accepting we just benefitted from an oil boom for 20 years! We have no buffer for any future shock to the economy. Who knows what will hit us next?"

Damien's stream of consciousness moved on. "I do sympathise with the environmentalists' desire to wean ourselves off fossil fuels. But I found the Scottish Green lady, Judy Lamb's, argument naïve. I don't think that stopping Scotland's North Sea Oil production or investment will make the slightest difference to the amount of fossil fuel used in the world in the next 30 years. We are just the 21st oil producer in the world! If we shut it all down tomorrow, at least 5 of the 50 major oil producing countries will gladly absorb the demand. The States, Saudi and Russia each produce over 12 times the UK's production. They can easily fill the gap. The States alone increased oil production by over 3 million barrels a day in a very short timeframe. Libya and Iran are desperate to increase their production, to name just two eager nations. In fact, it would make it even worse for the environment. We'd need to transport imported oil from further afield and add extra CO_2 emissions!"

"That's all very well," Michael rebutted. "But someone needs to take a lead in the world, and we can't duck it just because we're small. My question is more about whether the ordinary person in the street is willing to give up any of their wealth to do so. That's what's needed until we have the alternative. Look at Denmark. After 15 years of heavy investment and subsidies renewables still only account for 3% of their economy. How is Scotland to replace 8% of its GDP dependent on oil and gas, and by when?"

"That's my point", said Damien, "Oil and gas created 240,000 highly paid jobs in Scotland. Think how much tax that generates! How many jobs have been produced from renewables thus far? 2,500 jobs in onshore wind farms. A far cry from 240,000. Denmark seems to have come to a good balance, continuing to encourage further investment in oil and gas to help pay for the heavy investment in renewable technology. Denying a trillion pounds of future wealth that could be the funding for renewable research and forestation seems crazy, even for the ardent environmentalist."

Michael smiled. "But the environmentalists are right to ask for a major change. It will be interesting to see how the politicians in the world handle the need for an extra $100bn investment to make even a small dent on the temperature rise. Are Labour or the Tories going to impose a heavy carbon tax on travel to fund it when all the voluntary offset schemes are basically a flop? Twenty pence[7] on the price of a litre of petrol? Forty euros extra on the price of a holiday ticket to Spain? Good luck to those who want elected!"

"Look at Norway," added Damien, "High price restaurants and coffee, anti-consumption, jam tomorrow not today, high income taxes, great quality of life. Do you think the Scottish public or even the environmentalists are ready for that?"

"My son and his partner in Edinburgh certainly are. They want Scotland to be more like Norway, and to have lots more trees!"

Just as the two economists were settling into a predictable pattern of debate, in walked Patrick Kluivert, the newly elected Green MEP from the Netherlands and namesake of the famous footballer. He was snatching a quick coffee before heading back home to the Hague for the weekend.

"Hi Michael and Damien, good conference. But hey, what a heat today! Who's going to try telling me now that global warming isn't happening? And when are you two going to wake up and smell the coffee. The industry's still in denial – but the millennials are going to be unstoppable. You've got your heads in the sand. The price fall in 2016 knocked the stuffing out of the industry, and surely no-one seriously believes that oil will recover to its former glory.

"It's sad to see a great country such as Scotland fail to invest enough in its incredible opportunities for renewables. You've a weak national utility plan as far as I can see. You're dominated by foreign-owned utility companies with no real interest in Scottish industry or jobs, let alone enough drive to create a massive renewable export business. As for Scotland's transport policy – it looks to me to be just contributing to HS2 and Crossrail. And you are so wound up about Brexit and politics you are not getting on with it. When are you going to get your act together and save the planet?"

Damien teased him as Patrick rushed out with his coffee slopping around dangerously in his reusable cup. "Catching a taxi to St Pancras Eurostar I presume, rather than using your bike or walking for 30 minutes in the summer heat?"

"Yes, I ordered an electric taxi. So, your problem is? You guys really are going to find yourselves on the wrong side of history. The only question is, how soon?"

Things can change very suddenly

In the 1970's the oil boom came to Scotland, creating over 100,000 well paid jobs. In 2008-9 tax revenues[8] from Scotland's geographic share of oil revenue peaked at over £8 billion. In 2013-14, overall UK tax take on North Sea Oil was £4.5 billion. In 2014, oil wealth from tax revenues and jobs was a key element of the SNP's prospectus for independence. Better Together, however, claimed that Scotland's oil would run out within a few years.

In 2015, the USA became self-sufficient in oil again, thanks to dramatic technological breakthroughs in directional drilling and fracking. As a result, the government repealed its law banning oil exports and flooded the market with new oil from its domestic production.

In 2016 oil prices collapsed from over $100 to under $30 per barrel. Many of the higher cost producers worldwide were driven out of the market. Scottish oil production slumped. Scotland's oil revenues collapsed. Tax take dropped by nearly 99% to £60 million. Many jobs were lost. Aberdeen's boom times were over – or were they?

In 2017-18, the oil price rose again, as is the way of volatile commodity markets. Scottish oil production picked up. BP's Schiehallion field west of Shetland re-opened after a major upgrade. Scotland's oil flowed again, though not at previous levels. The Oil and Gas Authority estimated that 12 billion more barrels could be extracted from the UK continental shelf by 2050, worth up to £1 trillion.

By 2018 annual tax take recovered to £1.2 billion. That's probably as good as it will get from now on, because under the terms of their drilling licences, the oil companies will get refunds on the tax they've already paid when they incur the cost of decommissioning their exhausted oil fields.

In early 2020, a vicious oil price war broke out among the big exporters in response to the glut from the growth of US domestic production. The Covid-19 pandemic then brought the global economy to a shuddering halt. Chaos hit the markets. The Texas oil price went negative for the first time in its history.

In May 2020, clean skies over Delhi, Seoul and Mumbai offered an exciting glimpse of what the world could look like. Images of clear blue sky behind the Taj Mahal will be remembered for a long time.

At the same time, investors worry that oil and gas reserves are becoming "stranded assets." In June 2020, BP and Shell wrote down the value of their assets by $40 billion. There is growing pressure not to return to the old normal, and instead to make use of the massive amounts of money governments are spending to stimulate their economies after the pandemic to accelerate the green transition.

Scotland is a high-cost producer. Without radical breakthroughs in offshore technologies, we won't be able to stay in the oil export market till the end. It is wise to transition out while our oil can still be sold at a profit, to generate the cash we need to make a good green transition and cover the decommissioning costs. Whether we have ten years, twenty or thirty we don't know. We certainly are unlikely to have fifty. By the time we get to 2070, where our vision is focused, Scotland is unlikely to be producing economically significant amounts of oil.

The Greta Thunberg effect

The physics of global warming was already well understood back in the 1970s. Then, from the 1980s onwards, the topic became increasingly politicised. Arguments about the human contribution to climate change escalated. When President Trump was elected in 2016, the debate became heated. In 2017, he announced that the USA would withdraw from the Paris Climate Accord.

One Friday in August 2018, a 15-year-old Swedish schoolgirl sat alone outside the Swedish Parliament. She went back every Friday, taking time off school, to sit there alone.

Photographs of her went viral, and her influence gradually increased. In 2019, millions of schoolkids joined climate strikes all over the world.

In August 2019, Greta Thunberg addressed world leaders at the UN Climate Action Summit in New York. Chastised by our children, more of us are waking up to the urgency of climate action.

Things are indeed changing very suddenly, and we need to learn to adapt.

Is there a problem?

2019 was the warmest year on record across the world. Wildfires devastated large areas of California and eastern Australia. Scotland declared a climate emergency. Many other nations and local governments followed suit.

In 2020 the level of carbon dioxide (CO_2) in the atmosphere is the highest for three million years. In spite of all the progress with renewable energy, atmospheric CO_2 is still increasing, just not quite as fast. Methane, a much stronger but less long-lasting greenhouse gas, is increasing faster.

Global average surface temperature remains on track to exceed pre-industrial levels by 1.5 degrees in the next couple of decades.

This is a big problem for all of humanity, and for all the ecosystems we depend on.

Why is that?

The climate has been unusually stable for the last 10,000 years. It was this unusual stability that allowed complex human societies to develop. We simply don't know exactly what will happen if the current rate of warming continues; but we can be certain that it won't be good. And it will happen, unless drastic action is taken, not just to stop additional human emissions of greenhouse gases, but also to draw down the excess CO_2 we have already pumped into the atmosphere in the form of industrial emissions for the past two hundred years.

Between 1960 and 2015, annual human-caused CO_2 emissions tripled, from 20 billion tonnes to 60 billion tonnes[9]. And in spite of all the hype we hear from politicians, emissions continue almost unabated.

How are we putting all this CO_2 into the atmosphere? The main contributors worldwide[10] are:

Cause	% of human-caused CO_2 emissions
coal	40%;
oil	34%;
gas	21%;
cement	4%;
flaring	1%

What else are we putting into the atmosphere? One of the biggest issues is methane (natural gas), burped by cows and leaked from gas wells and pipelines. Methane emissions are much lower than CO_2 emissions in volume terms, and the gas doesn't persist for as long in the atmosphere – but while it does, its warming effect is much stronger. Methane matters, and it will matter more as CO_2 emissions are reduced. The world needs to get to net zero emissions by 2050, and to draw down a lot of the carbon in the atmosphere by 2100, if we are to avoid inflicting climate chaos on future generations. (Ignore the alarmist suggestions that the human race might die out. It can survive climate chaos, though not in its current numbers, and with severely disrupted lifestyle.)

It's useful to slice the data another way, and to include the effect of other greenhouse gases as well as CO_2[11]:

Industry Sector	% contribution to all human-caused greenhouse gas emissions
Energy, including electricity and heat	35%
Agriculture, forestry and other land use	24%
Industry	21%
Transport	14%
Building	6%

Methane matters

Those burping cows are making a big contribution to global warming. Cutting back on cow and sheep meat and dairy would mark a big and quick reduction in emissions. This is also why, when the oil and chemical industries vent off methane, they set fire to it. As bad as all that flaring is at the gas plant at Mossmorran in Fife – sometimes from Edinburgh it can look like the fires of Mordor glowing in the distance – the global warming effect would be much worse if the methane was vented straight into the atmosphere without being burnt.

Not only is methane much worse in its greenhouse effect than CO_2, but to cap it all, its effect over the next thirty years, the period in which it's desirable to bring greenhouse gas emissions to net zero, is not properly accounted for in countries' calculated emissions. It's even worse than the numbers suggest.

Only read this bit if you care about numbers

The effect of other gases is factored into the global warming sums using a strange-sounding unit called the 'Megatonne of CO_2-equivalent', or $MtCO_2(e)$.

If a given amount of a given gas has the same global warming effect as a million tonnes of CO_2 (over a defined period, usually taken as 100 years), then the emissions of that amount of that gas are counted as 1 $MtCO_2(e)$. So 1 $MtCO_2(e)$ means "emissions with a global warming effect equivalent to a million tonnes of CO_2." You see why scientists use abbreviations.

It's like a Tog rating for a duvet. Imagine you have a very expensive duvet made of an exotic material that's a very good insulator. It's very thin, very light, and still has a Tog rating of ten – suitable for spring and autumn in Scotland. Let's say it is 5 cm thick and weighs 500 grams. A cheap duvet with the same Tog rating would keep you equally warm, but it would be much thicker and heavier – maybe 30 cm thick and weighing five or ten kilograms. The Tog rating allows us to compare duvets of different materials and thicknesses, by ignoring what they're made of, and concentrating on what they *do* – i.e. how well they keep us warm.

To be precise, it's the 'Global Warming Potential' or GWP of a gas that works like the 'Tog rating'. The GWP lets us compare the global warming effect of different greenhouse gases. For example, a given mass of CO_2 has a 'Tog rating' (GWP) of one. The same mass of methane is normally quoted as having a 'Tog rating' (GWP) of 25. Turning that round, it only takes one twenty-fifth as much methane as CO_2 to produce a given amount of global warming.

Usually GWP is calculated over a hundred-year period. But, because methane only stays in the atmosphere for a few decades, all the warming effect of methane happens over those first few decades after it's released. The figure usually used for the global warming potential of methane is 25 over 100 years; but if you recalculate it for a 20-year period instead, it's 84. This means that, though there is only $1/200$ as much methane as CO_2 in the atmosphere, it has about a third of the global warming effect over a 20-year period.

It's as if a well-wisher tucked Sleeping Beauty up under a duvet they believed was 25 Tog, which would keep her comfortable for her 100-year sleep. But it was actually 84 Togs when new, so at first she'd get far too hot; and then it evaporated within twenty years, so that she'd freeze for the rest of her hundred-year sleep.

The methane story has a sting in the tail. Vast amounts of methane are frozen into the arctic tundra in northern Russia and Canada. What happens if global warming continues, the tundra thaws, and all this methane is released into the atmosphere? It could increase the amount of atmospheric methane by a factor of twelve[12]. The exceptionally hot summer in northern Russia in 2020 is an ominous warning. The IPCC[13] forecasts are not worst case. They don't allow for unpredictable tipping points such as this one. This is why the scientific advice is to stop our carbon emissions as quickly as we possibly can.

Scotland's story (though only on emissions!)

Scotland's greenhouse gas emissions have halved since 1990, which is good going. But that's probably the easy half. We need to eliminate the other half in the next 25 years to achieve the Scottish Government's ambition for the country to be net zero by 2045.

And some of our emissions are merely being exported, not actually eliminated. The figures don't include the carbon other countries emit to make the stuff we buy from them, nor to run the data centres that service our internet use. Much of the 10 million tonne reduction in industry emissions between 1990 and 2016 is because we offshored more manufacturing and the associated carbon emissions. In particular, the Ravenscraig steelworks was shut down in 1993, and we now import all of our steel, mainly from Poland and China.

Again, skip this bit if you don't like numbers!

In 2017 Scotland emitted 40.5 million tonnes of CO_2-equivalent emissions, down from 76.3 $MtCO_2(e)$ in 1990[14]. The relative amounts of the different sectors are shown in Fig. 4.1, below[15].

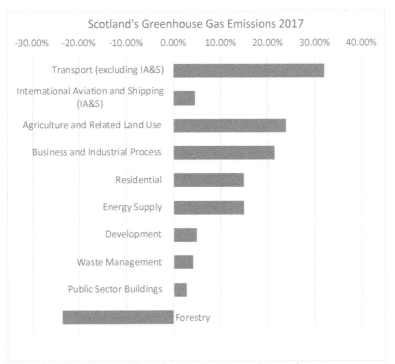

Transport makes the biggest contribution, with surface transport accounting for 2/3 of the total. It's not planes, but cars and lorries, that emit the most. The "energy" (i.e. electricity) sector has reduced its emissions by ¾ since 1990, thanks to the phasing out of coal and the increase in renewables. We still burn natural gas in power stations when the wind isn't blowing hard enough.

Agriculture and related land use caused 9.7 MtCO$_2$(e) of emissions. About half of this is methane, mainly from burping livestock. Another quarter is nitrous oxide from fertiliser. Forestry absorbed 9.5 MtCO$_2$(e), almost entirely offsetting the impact of agriculture.

Power generation (marked as energy supply in Fig. 4.1) in Scotland has been considerably decarbonised since 1990, mainly by shutting down our coal fired power stations and building lots of wind farms. That continues apace, though the 2018 figures show an uptick in emissions because the Hunterston nuclear power station was shut down for some of the year, and we had to burn more gas at Inverkip and Peterhead to make up the shortfall.

Residential buildings emit the same again as electricity, mainly because of gas used for heating and cooking. Better insulation would make a big difference to this number.

What can and should Scotland do about it?

The Scottish Government has set a goal of net zero carbon emissions by 2045. It would be good to achieve this sooner, and that's not impossible. As we have noted, things can change very suddenly.

It's the way of technological and social change to muddle along for ages without much happening, then suddenly take off when the time is ripe. That time is ripe for renewables. Thanks to increased production volumes and better technology, the price of wind and solar, and now batteries as well, has come down so much that renewables are winning auctions for grid-scale guaranteed despatch electricity supply contracts without any need for subsidy. (Guaranteed despatch means being able to supply power on demand 24/7, not just when the wind is blowing or the sun shining.) The shift to renewables now seems unstoppable.

There are three important issues. First, what to do with the rest of our oil? Second, how to make the most of the massive opportunity presented by a worldwide shift to zero-carbon economies? And third, how best to spend our money and resources to reduce our emissions, as individuals and as a nation and planet?

These issues are an opportunity for Scotland, not a problem. Scotland is estimated to have 25% of the EU's potential wind and tidal power, and 10% of wave power potential[16] — possibly up to 60 GW potential capacity, compared with a peak domestic demand of about 5 GW[17]. We really can be a net energy exporter in a carbon-free world.

There is a lot of talk about using biomass for energy. Biomass is stuff like wood, typically processed into wood pellets and burnt in power stations instead of coal. There are serious problems with using biomass for electricity. Biomass uses an incredible amount of land to produce a given amount of electrical energy sustainably; and in terms of particulate emissions, it's worse than diesel cars. There is far too much abuse of the system, unscrupulous companies and countries chopping down forests willy-nilly and certifying wood products as renewable when they absolutely are not. Scotland should certainly not be importing any wood for biomass. And where biomass may be the best low-carbon alternative to gas for heating our homes and workplaces[18], we should grow and process our own, guaranteed renewable and zero-carbon.

How much of our oil should we leave in the ground?

This is — literally — the sixty-four-billion-dollar question.

Climate activists argue that "all remaining fossil fuel need to be kept in the ground." This is broadly true, based on the scientific evidence. "But what about the workers?" you ask. The oil and gas industries still provide 100,000 well paid jobs in Scotland[19]. Their unmanaged decline would destroy livelihoods and reduce tax revenue. Still, according to some recent studies[20], it's possible to fully replace the economic contribution of the oil and gas industry by betting on renewable energy — if the government does its job right. There certainly needs to be a managed transition, to avoid economic collapse and massive social disruption. Imagine if all those workers furloughed during the Covid-19 lockdown had been paid to work on new green technologies!

There are more subtle issues too.

If Scotland went into 'hair shirt' mode, and unilaterally stopped pumping and using oil tomorrow, would it have any effect on the climate crisis? The answer is, certainly not a lot, and possibly none at all. Our emissions are but a small part of the world's total. The shortfall in production would be made up by Saudi Arabia, Russia, Iran and onshore US producers without batting an eyelid. They are desperate to increase their own production and as a result of the recent cutbacks in world demand they have plenty capacity to do so. Co-ordinated international action to keep long-term demand low as well as constraining supply is the only way to avoid climate chaos.

What if, on a point of principle, we kept our own oil in the ground, and bought from others the remaining oil we'll need until we've gone completely green? Our carbon footprint might actually increase, because of the additional transport. And there's a strategic aspect as well. If we depend on imports from volatile parts of the world, we and our neighbours can be held to ransom by the remaining oil suppliers, or by those who can interrupt the sea lanes. For as long as we need oil and gas, it makes sense to use our own and not depend on imports.

Some argue that there's no rush, that we should wait for others, that we are too small to make any difference. However, there are good reasons to accelerate the transition. Quite apart from the fact that we promised we would – we declared a climate crisis, and we committed to achieve net zero by 2045 – there are hard technical and economic reasons to start our green transition now, ambitiously, and without delay.

It costs more to extract oil from deep under the Atlantic than from shallow oil reservoirs under the desert. In price wars, countries like Saudi Arabia can drive the price down to a level at which they would still make a profit, but we'd be selling our oil at a loss. Electric cars will replace petrol and diesel ones. Renewables will replace diesel for off-grid users. Ships will become more efficient, with carbon-free ammonia fuel expected to replace fuel oil. Even some planes will switch to electric or hydrogen power. The demand for oil will change dramatically, and not necessarily very predictably. Renewables are replacing fossil fuels for power generation much faster than many industry experts expected. This is bringing prices of renewable energy down very rapidly, making it ever more competitive, which accelerates the trend even more. Every year the International Energy Agency, biased by US thinking, is having to revise its renewable energy forecasts – always upwards.

Do we need to realise the green transition yet?

The countries and organisations that do best out of the green energy transition will be those who invest at the right time.

It has been the right time for over ten years already.

The remaining oil and gas revenue can be used to finance the switch to green and to build a strong and sustainable export sector. Our surplus electricity can be used to produce hydrogen for our own use and export, and export directly to near neighbours. We can earn carbon credits for sequestering our and other people's carbon emissions, in our trees and our peat bogs, and in our expired oil and gas reservoirs, using carbon capture and storage. If we make the right investments at the right scale and rate, we can sell both products and technologies to other countries to help them also move quickly and cost-effectively away from fossil fuels.

Scotland was a world leader in wind turbines in the 1980s. The Thatcher government stopped supporting the development, and Denmark jumped in to become the world leader in wind energy. Most of the structures for the new windfarm off the Forth Estuary will be built in Indonesia. Most of the profits will go to EDF, the French state-owned energy company. Industrial policy at its worst. We'll get some work – maybe (even that is in doubt as we go to print) – but nothing remotely like what was expected. Conventional solar and wind generators are now mature technologies, commodity items built by the cheapest global supplier. (Hint: because we didn't invest at the right time in the right way, that's not us.)

There is no point in Scotland trying to make conventional wind turbines in competition with others who are already producing the complex turbines themselves very efficiently. But there's no point shaving a few pounds off the construction cost of multi-billion-pound windfarms to spend all the money saved, and more, on welfare benefits for people in Scotland who could have earned a decent wage doing much of the work[21]. We need an industrial policy and public procurement rules that ensure as much as possible of the general engineering, final assembly and installation work for renewable energy installations, and all of the maintenance and servicing, are done in Scotland with Scottish labour. As we'll discuss at the end of the chapter, contrary to popular belief, this would NOT contravene EU or WTO state aid rules.

It would also be wise to exploit our abundant wind to be a net energy exporter – a powerhouse for the British Isles and near Europe. And there is a great deal to be gained by investing to make the next disruptive jump in wind power technology, whatever that might be.

How about wave and tidal power? We've been struggling with wave power for thirty years. It's a really hard engineering problem, and maybe it's just not going to happen. Tidal power looks much more promising. It's more predictable, uses more familiar technology (basically a ship propeller and power plant run backwards), and our waters are some of the most suitable in the world. Unfortunately, we have again let the lead pass to other countries, notably Norway and potentially Ireland and Canada, but we're not so far behind. Maybe there is still time to catch up, or to team with the leaders to co-develop the best technology and bring it to full-scale production. Our vision includes an expansion of the research and development in this technology, and not letting the intellectual property or the high-value-added aspects of manufacturing drift abroad.

What's going to happen in the next thirty years? A recent report by Morgan Stanley suggests that getting the world to net zero by 2050 will require $50 trillion of investment, split, they suggest, as follows:

- Carbon Capture and Storage 5%

- Biofuels (mainly bioethanol for cars and aviation) 6%

- Electric vehicles 22%

- Renewable power generation (mainly solar and wind) 28%

- Hydrogen 39%

The amount of money involved sounds mind-boggling; but as the Heriot Watt University's Professor Andreas Busch pointed out[22], this is just 2% of world GDP, the same amount the world's governments will spend on defence in that period. And the world's governments are at the time of writing planning to spend nearly 20% of that figure[23] – $9 trillion – on rescuing their economies from Covid-19 in the space of a few months. So why not spend *all* of that on the low-carbon transition? Nearly 20% of the required funding has suddenly become available, this year, just like that!

It's entirely doable if the will is there.

Indeed, the $50 trillion figure potentially overestimates the requirement, since it does not capture saving energy by making our systems more efficient – for example by improving house insulation, and passive ventilation to reduce the energy needed for heating and air conditioning. On the other hand, global energy demand continues to increase as developing countries aspire to first-world quality of life. For developing countries, there is a direct correlation between energy use and life expectancy[24].

So, what could Scotland focus on?

A lot of money will be spent on – and earned from – decommissioning the North Sea Oil and Gas installations when they get to the end of their lives. The amount involved is estimated at upwards of £40Bn[25]. Legally, this liability rests with the people who are operating the assets when they get to the end of their life. However, because of the terms within the contracts with the producers, the taxpayer has ended up with more than 50% of the liability, given that the operators can claim rebates on Petroleum Revenue Tax paid in previous years to partially offset the decommissioning costs. Thus, decommissioning is a double-edged sword. On the one hand it's a business opportunity – one the Norwegians are taking more advantage of than we are at the moment. On the other hand, it's a liability for the taxpayer – currently running at £500 million a year, and likely to peak at over a billion pounds a year. How to allocate this liability between Scotland and the rest of the UK would be one of many vexed issues to be argued over if we were to move to a different constitutional settlement in future, be it independence or federalism.

Other opportunities in and around decommissioning include the use of suitable spent oil and gas fields for Carbon Capture and Storage (CCS). There's increasing opposition to storing compressed CO_2 under inhabited land, because of the risks of earthquakes and leakage. Scotland has a large fraction of Europe's potential offshore CCS capacity. In principle we can use the existing subsea infrastructure to pump captured CO_2 into the geological formations that held the oil and gas. Yet, there are still many practical issues that need detailed geological and engineering assessment, and industrial-scale demonstration projects, before we'll know if this is really a viable option. On the plus side, we have the expertise to do this in the Scottish Universities and offshore industry.

As well as the huge installations of wind power, Scotland has got experimental and early production projects in: hydrogen (produced using otherwise wasted excess wind power in Orkney): electric vehicle infrastructure; proof-of-concept commercial electric flights (Orkney, scheduled for 2021); grid-scale demonstrations of tidal power (also Orkney); and various forms of biofuel.

The issue with biofuels, as with biomass, is that the energy conversion efficiency from sunlight to the vegetation that is used as raw material is very low. Only a minute fraction (possibly as little as 1/10,000) of the sunlight landing on a field ends up as useful energy in biofuel. If biofuels are to provide world-scale benefits, they also cause world-scale environmental destruction: witness the current concern about destruction of tropical rain forests in Indonesia to make space for palm oil plantations, spurred on by EU subsidies.

In Scotland we have the potential to generate something approaching ten times as much renewable electricity as we need for domestic consumption. This excess energy can be sold directly, if suitable long-distance connectors are built; or used to power totally new industries, such as carbon-free manufacture of hydrogen and ammonia fuel – ammonia is currently the favoured carbon-free fuel for merchant shipping[26] – and for other energy intensive industries such as aluminium smelting, and computer data centres.

So, what *should* Scotland focus on?

If we want to take advantage of this potential, a business-as-usual laissez-faire approach won't do it.

We think Scotland should make three strategic investments in renewable energy and technology:

1. Ensuring we meet our own net zero target by 2045;

2. Selling our surplus clean energy and carbon capture and storage capacity to our near neighbours;

3. Investing in innovative future renewables technologies for sale as intellectual property, and also as manufactured products and support services, to the world market.

If we are to make this a success, the transition needs to be planned and led strategically, at large scale, and fast. We recommend the 'moon shot' mentality as advocated by economic advisor to the Scottish Government, Mariana Mazzucato[27], who champions the 'mission-oriented' approach to managing this sort of endeavour[28]: strong commitment to challenging measurable goals, within a tight but achievable time frame; top-down vision and strategy, allied with lots of bottom-up experimentation; tolerance of risk and failure; and placing enough bets that some of them will come through.

And don't forget, state aid is allowed for this sort of strategic shift. "State aid might be necessary and justified to address a market failure, as when SMEs have difficulties finding investment capital. It may also be necessary to achieve policy goals such as regional economic development or environmental protection. Governments can, for instance, use state aid to stimulate businesses to invest in less developed areas or advanced environmentally friendly technologies."[29] Every single one of these points applies.

The Scottish Government is making the right noises. But policies are not enough. Only all shoulders to the wheel will make it happen.

References for Chapter 4

[1] NOAA, the USA's National Oceanic and Atmospheric Administration
[2] BP Statistical Review of World Energy 2019
[3] MIT Technology Review, Kevin Bullis, 2008
[4] https://www.bloomberg.com/news/articles/2018-12-04/fridman-s-dea-agrees-largest-oil-deal-since-mexico-opened-up
[5] IPPR Commission on Economic Justice, Our Common Wealth, A Citizen's Wealth Fund for the UK, April 2018

---

[6] WTI (West Texas Intermediate) is a grade of crude oil used as a benchmark in oil pricing. (Wikipedia)

[7] Or $200/tonne of CO_2 equivalent emission. This is the level required to seriously drive down carbon emissions, according to the MIT Carbon Simulator.

[8] https://www.gov.scot/publications/government-expenditure-revenue-scotland-2017-18/pages/4/

[9] 'Decarbonise or revolutionise' - Professor Andreas Busch, Inaugural Lecture, Heriot Watt University, 20/11/19

[10] Global Carbon Project data for 2018, slightly adjusted to account for apparent rounding errors. https://www.globalcarbonproject.org/carbonbudget/19/files/GCP_CarbonBudget_2019.pdf

[11] Global Sustainable Development report, UN, 2019

[12] https://en.wikipedia.org/wiki/Arctic_methane_emissions

[13] IPCC – Intergovernmental Panel on Climate Change, the international body set up by governments to assess and summarise scientific evidence on climate change.

[14] Reducing emissions in Scotland, 2019 Progress Report to Parliament. Committee on Climate Change Dec. 2019

[15] Data from https://www.gov.scot/publications/scottish-greenhouse-gas-emissions-2017/pages/3/

[16] https://en.wikipedia.org/wiki/Renewable_energy_in_Scotland#Realisation_of_the_potential – old figures, possibly from 2005.

[17] A GW, or Gigawatt, is a billion watts, or a million kilowatts. A typical electric kettle consumes 3 kilowatts. Scotland's electricity demand is like 1-1.5 million electric kettles constantly boiling away.

[18] Common Weal certainly think so, if combined with solar thermal: https://commonweal.scot/our-common-home/heating

[19] https://oilandgasuk.cld.bz/Workforce-Report-2019/8/

[20] See for example https://platformlondon.org/2019/09/17/oil-jobs-scotland-renewables/

[21] https://sourcenews.scot/why-is-scotlands-green-energy-manufacturing-industry-in-crisis-in-a-climate-emergency/

[22] during his Inaugural Lecture (Heriot Watt University, 20/11/19)

[23] International Energy Agency – Sustainable Recovery – world energy outlook special report – June 2020.

[24] Czech/Canadian economist Vaclav Smil estimates a minimum energy requirement of 3.5 kilowatt per capita for a high human development index: in, we think, *Energy in Nature and Society: General Energetics of Complex Systems*, *The MIT Press*, Cambridge, 2008

[25] Energy Voice, *Decommissioning cost efforts 'compromised' by 5% of North Sea operators, says OGA*, 19th August 2020

[26] https://vpoglobal.com/2019/07/27/energy-experts-support-carbon-free-ammonia-as-a-marine-fuel/

[27] Mazzucato M, The Entrepreneurial State, Anthem 2013, Random House 2018

[28] https://marianamazzucato.com/research/mission-oriented-innovation-policy/

[29] House of Commons Library: EU State Aid rules and WTO Subsidies Agreement https://commonslibrary.parliament.uk/research-briefings/sn06775/

Chapter 5

Making Healthcare Fit for the Future

"Cure sometimes, treat often and comfort always."

Hippocrates

"Assisting surgeries, disinfecting rooms, dispensing medication, keeping company: believe it or not these are the tasks medical robots will soon undertake in hospitals, pharmacies, or your nearest doctor's office."

The Medical Futurist

Any country, especially one with an ageing population such as Scotland, must make the most of its healthcare sector. Otherwise it will never be healthy, wealthy and wise. Scotland, with its proud history of medical innovation and its well-respected NHS, is positioned to take advantage of this long term, high growth, profitable market sector. If the last 50 years were the era of a healthy heart, then the next 50 years are about investing in a healthy brain. Further opportunities arise from revamping the 'primary care' sector, encouraging consumer medical technology into the homes and hands of the people, dealing with the growing mental health issues, making the Public Health and Care Home sectors fit for purpose, and creating larger scale, Scottish-headquartered biomedical service and equipment companies.

Yet, no amount of investment in healthcare will solve the deeper problems of society caused by loneliness, and a deficit of hope and purpose in peoples' lives. That can only come from a renewal of body, mind, and spirit. To be healthy, the nation also needs to be wealthy and wise, topics addressed throughout this book.

What just happened to the world?

The early morning sky was a deep purple as we awoke. We finished a brisk breakfast before picking up our cases to travel by taxi to Aviemore station through what remained of the ancient Caledonian forest. The air was still, and the winter chill was made worse by our wearing summer clothes for our long journey ahead. We boarded the train for London and settled into our seats, as we had done many times before. The eight-hour journey was uneventful, and the train slid into King's Cross with swiss clock precision. The uber to Heathrow was the usual, painfully slow crossing of a bustling London. Our work in the United Arab Emirates beckoned, and the British Airways flight to Abu Dhabi, almost full, was the last part of our journey. Everything was operating as normal, but there was a real tension in the air.

The difference hit us visibly as soon as we landed, the tension that we had perceived in the air suddenly becoming reality on the ground. Temperature cameras greeted us on arrival, first installed in late January to test arrivals from China. Ambulances were on standby. Cameras also appeared a few days later in the lobby entry of our small apartment block on Al Maryah Island, one of the many islands that forms Abu Dhabi. They blinked at us again in our two local shops, which, to the surprise of some of our UK family members, are Waitrose and Boots. The drama had been triggered in the United Arab Emirates by an infected Wuhan Chinese family in Dubai in early February, followed by positive tests on two Italians attending a cycling tour in Abu Dhabi. Six hundred people from the same hotel were quarantined and tested. 'Test and Trace' was well underway. Schools closed on the 8th March, the day we landed. Our friends, whose son and daughter, Daniel and Isabel, attend Cranleigh School, twinned with the English school of the same name, were setting up their home-schooling routine. By the third week of March, the borders were closed, malls and mosques shut. A nightly curfew and street disinfection regime came into force alongside widespread testing. The UAE had imposed a strict lockdown on its 8 million people, with heavy fines for non-compliance. The MERS emergency in 2012 and previous pandemics had been a good rehearsal for this outbreak.

By the time we made our next trip to the UK in May on an empty Etihad flight, mandatory masks and clammy gloves had become part of our normal routine. The return trip to the UAE via Frankfurt on Lufthansa was even more complicated, and demonstrated the more casual attitude in the UK. This time, a formal application to the UAE Government was required to regain access. A negative Covid test by the UAE-approved test centre in Glasgow was mandatory within 96 hours of boarding the plane. A second Covid test was required on landing in Abu Dhabi, followed by a walk through a disinfection tunnel and a tedious spell in the crowded arrivals lounge before being released from the airport. And finally, we returned to a 14-day, strictly policed, quarantine regime in our one-bedroom apartment, totally reliant on Zoom calls and delivery of food and medicine to our door.

Within a short period of 6 months, the world had become a very different place.

The demands on Healthcare were already high.

Even before the Covid-19 crisis, every nation in the world was already dissatisfied with its healthcare system and was on a continuous path to deal with shortcomings. After all, humans have an insatiable appetite for the extension of life with an ailment-free existence. The pandemic has simply brought the shortfalls of existing healthcare systems into much sharper focus, and added to the already long list of demands placed on these:

- Extreme pressure from the ageing population in the West. The longer we live and the more we cure, the greater the self-generated demand for more care.

- Extra requests from the younger online generation who are used to instant access to all goods and services.

- Further investment in high-speed broadband coverage, digitisation, and new technologies to enhance traditional medical practices.

- Increased demand for alternative ways to control infections as antimicrobial resistance increases.

- Added pressure from a rise in demand for better health from the increasing wealth in large countries such as China, India and Brazil.

- A growth in world population until 2070 – 141 million babies born every year worldwide, as opposed to 56 million deaths – and an ageing population for centuries thereafter. A trend started much earlier in the West.

- Increased regional pressure from mass migration. In 2019, 71 million persons in the world were displaced, including 26 million living in so-called temporary refugee camps.

- A new "Silk Road" from India and China to import cheaper, outsourced medical supplies.

- A rise in blame and litigation culture, reinforced by social media. Perfection expected, risk aversion increased, and added legal costs causing a distraction from front-line services.

- A societal demand for lower levels of avoidable death. Safer cars, anti-smoking, and anti-military campaigns as the avoidable deaths nations are willing to tolerate decrease from millions to thousands, if not to hundreds.

- And now, a world economy on its knees from the spread of a highly infectious disease that has disrupted the lives of the vast majority of seven billion humans on the planet.

To control this insatiable demand for more and better, governments and healthcare providers have imposed a wide range of controls so as to prevent medical care becoming an unaffordable burden on the country's economy. They have employed queuing systems, price controls, delegation of resource allocation to medics, individual fees – full or partial – and the use of insurance discipline, to control spending. They have also encouraged businesses to create wealth from the sector in order to relieve some of the economic burden.

The UK has focussed on financial targets and controls as it raised funding for the NHS, pre-financial crash, to meet more acceptable international levels. Not surprising, given these pressures. The focus on centralisation, rationalisation, IT systems, bed productivity, and reducing hospitalisation is largely aimed at improving productivity for the sake of governments and healthcare providers, and much less for patients' needs.

The Challenge of Creating a 50-year Vision for Healthcare

Given these immense short-term pressures, creating a vision for healthcare is a major challenge. However, it is more than simply these pressures that make it difficult. When faced with ill health we all struggle with the emotions of having to entrust our lives and those whom we love the most to healthcare providers. This vulnerability can make it hard to accept that there may not be a perfect outcome. The provider and recipient both have to be sensitive to this vulnerability. It is therefore with humility that we provide the reader with a broad international perspective and propose a convincing path for Scotland's healthcare system in the next fifty years. We cannot be overly prescriptive on the tactics to be used. Systems change, and new ideas are adopted. It is too complex an issue to tackle in a single chapter. Many others have dedicated whole books to the subject. If our recommendations diminish in any way the central idea of service being at the heart of the healthcare sector, then we will have done the country a disservice.

We have looked at healthcare from three different angles. First of all, we have reviewed comparative international studies conducted by academics, medics, and commentators on the current state of UK and Scottish healthcare, including early learnings from Covid-19. Secondly, we have thrown our own personal experience into the mix. Everyone has their personal 'lived experience' of healthcare. Two of the authors have been involved in the medical world for many decades. Finally, we have taken a stab at identifying where Scotland could take a lead in the big future healthcare trends. It is these 'healthcare marathons" that provide the largest opportunity for Scotland over a 50-year period.

Where does Scotland stand today?

Let's start with some global facts on health outcomes. Every year just under sixty million people die worldwide. Eighteen million (30%) die from cardiovascular disease, ten million

(17%) from cancers, seven million (12%) from respiratory diseases, and two and a half million (4%) from dementia. These, and car deaths at about three million per annum, are the main killers. Of course, media headlines tend to focus on smaller, more newsworthy events. For example, worldwide drug and alcohol deaths of just under four hundred thousand. Or a few thousand from terrorism, USA shootings, and natural disasters. All tragic, but a very small number in the big picture. War used to be a major killer, averaging 1 million every year in the 20th Century, of which 75% civilians. It's now down to about one hundred thousand per annum. The new war, the invisible global war of Covid-19, will end up above 1 million deaths in 2020.

Are the main causes of death in Scotland the same? Not entirely. Out of approximately 59,000 deaths in Scotland in 2018, cancers are the largest category at just over 27%. Cardio-vascular nearly 18%. Respiratory 12%. Dementia is a growing number at over 10%. Car deaths less than 1%. Drugs, approximately 2% and growing. Alcohol also approximately 2%, but declining. Covid-19 expected to be over 6% in 2020.

So how do we compare in health outcomes with the rest of the world? The UK stands at number twenty-three in the world at preventing serious health outcomes[1] Iceland, Norway, and the Netherlands come out on top, with France and Germany slightly ahead of the UK. When compared with an OECD peer group, the UK fares worse than the average on fourteen of the twenty-seven outcome measures, better on five.[2] These overall comparisons have to be viewed with caution. According to the Nuffield Institute, who have examined many healthcare rankings, "comparing healthcare quality across different countries is inherently difficult due to the challenges involved in collecting high quality and comparable data."[3] There are, however, good comparative figures on life expectancy, one of the major health outcomes. Life expectancy in Scotland, at about 79, is two years worse than England. Some studies suggest Scotland has the lowest and most slowly improving life expectancy in Western Europe, the widest inequalities, and higher rates of mortality amongst younger working ages.

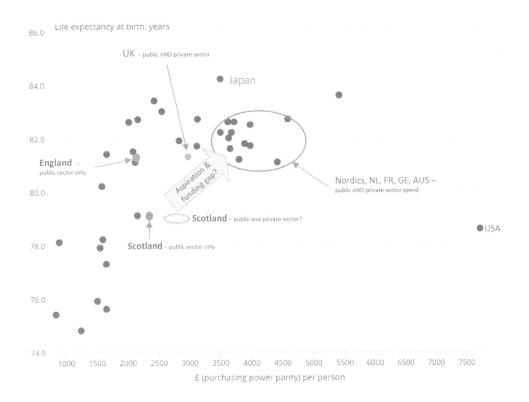

Figure 5.1 Life expectancy at birth, and current healthcare expenditure per person for OECD countries 2017. Figure adapted from ONS, "How does UK Healthcare Spending compare with other countries", Open Government Licence, 29 August 2019. Dotted ellipse for Scotland's 'public and private sector' spend is indicative; about 8.5% of Scottish population pays into private healthcare schemes.

If other success factors are considered, then the UK health system ranks much higher, as would Scotland's. For example, the US-based Commonwealth Fund[4] ranked the UK in the top three overall in comparison with eleven peer countries. In mental health it compares well, certainly when ranked by the narrower measures of severe illness and suicides[5]. The UK scores very highly on measures of administrative efficiency and delivering equitable and timely access to care, but it performs less well on health outcomes. Certainly, if we factor in productivity, especially with our lower numbers of medical staff per population, and compare healthcare spend to life expectancy, then the UK fares well – twice as effectively as the USA though still below the overall leader, Japan.

Other studies[6] have highlighted Scotland's reputation for strength in accident and emergency, and for the provision of a more personalised service with fewer layers of management. In contrast, Scotland struggles as a result of greater inequality in health outcomes, an increasingly ageing population relative to the rest of the UK, and geographical remoteness.

Scotland has a much higher number of hospitals (279) than other small nations in geographically sparse territories such as Norway (84) and Sweden (100). It also has a higher number of hospital beds per population than England, and equivalent to the average in Europe. On the surface, therefore, it has ample secondary care assets to cope as well as other leading nations. However, Scotland, as part of the UK, remains behind its main peers[7] in medical equipment spending, this accounting for a mere 0.31% of national GDP versus the peers' average of 0.51%.

In terms of academic reputation, the leading Scottish Medical School, Edinburgh University, ranks number thirty in the world versus the top three (Oxford, Cambridge, and Stanford), according to the Times World Ranking[8], and number nineteen according to the QS ranking[9]. And the nursing school is ranked by the QS comparisons[10] at number twenty-three compared with the top four rankings in the world of Pennsylvania, King's College London, John Hopkins, and Manchester. The ranking is important, despite being subjective and biased, because the league tables attract the best medical professionals and research from around the world, and help retain home grown talent.

Scotland's lobbyists, government officials, and university staff all point to the wonderful work being done in life sciences research and development. It's true. The life sciences industry in Scotland already employs over 40,000 people across 770 organisations, contributing in excess of £5.2 billion turnover and over £2 billion gross value added. This includes the pharmaceutical and medical equipment industries, which support over 5000 jobs. From 2009 to 2015 the sector created 170 life sciences start-ups, and over 60 life science spin outs from universities. 30% of the Scottish Investment Bank's investments are in life sciences.

Its venture capital structure in medical sciences is well-known throughout the UK. Scottish institutions capture 19% of the biosciences funding attracted by UK universities.

Scotland's determination to remain in a leading position in innovation is evidenced further by the multi-million-pound investments in the Scottish Precision Medicine Ecosystem and the Centre for Artificial Intelligence Research in Digital Diagnostics. It has established a brand new, world leading, Brain Research Scotland initiative in conjunction with the existing Scottish Dementia Research Centre, the Scottish Dementia Working Group, and National Dementia Carers Action Network. One of the authors was on the Edinburgh University Campaign Board that raised extra funding from private sources for the innovative concept of informatics, which combines computer science, psychology, artificial intelligence, and brain research. Nevertheless, complacency is dangerous. For example, the pharmaceutical industry contributes over £1.5 billion[11] to the Scottish economy, but it suffered a bit of a wobble from 2012 to 2017, with a drop in R&D spending and employment.

For a small country with limited resources there is a high risk of being spread far too thinly in pursuit of multiple opportunities. The digitisation of medicine has only just begun, and the list of innovations Scotland could be actively involved in is now very long. Just look at the multitude of potential medical opportunities highlighted in the 2019 Global Innovation Report (Table 5.1). Examples include continuous medical monitoring using smart eye lenses and many other body sensors; Augmented Reality (AR) and Virtual Reality (VR) moving from the gaming industry to medical schools, clinical and operating rooms; "digiceuticals" (using custom-designed software apps to guide the patient through healthcare and treatment regimens); personalized drugs; and robotic diagnosis and support. Artificial Intelligence and Big Data are in their infancy in the medical world, but we expect those to emerge in the next decade, assuming the issue of patient privacy can be addressed.

So, does Scotland already have a world-scale, broad-based research and development cluster to support a fifty-year vision for medical science? It is tempting to say yes, but the blunt answer is no. We would have answered yes at the time of the first world war, but it has since slipped down the world rankings. For example, in a review of the European scene, the Medical Device and Diagnostic Industry Report 2020 listed the top seven MediTech hubs in Europe: Grand Est in France; Medical Valley Nurnberg and Tuttlingen in Germany; Canton

Zurich in Switzerland; Emilia-Romagna in Italy, and the so-called Golden Triangle of London, Cambridge and Oxford.

Table 5.1: Promising fields for medical innovation and technologies[12]

NEW SCIENTIFIC BREAKTHROUGHS, TREATMENTS, AND CURES	
Genetics and stem cell research	Single-cell analysis Gene and stem cell therapies Genetic engineering and editing
Nanotechnology	Swallowable small devices
Biologics	Development and manufacture of complex biologics
Brain research, neurology, and neurosurgery	Characterization of the brain's major circuits New brain imagery for mental disorders Migraine treatment
New generation of vaccines and immunotherapy	HIV and universal flu vaccine Cancer vaccine Immunotherapy New vaccine delivery methods
Pain management	Effective, non-addictive medicines for pain management
Mental health treatments	Pre-symptomatic diagnosis and treatment of Alzheimer's disease and other cognitive declines
NEW MEDICAL TECHNOLOGIES	
Medical devices	3D printing Cardiac devices Implants and bionics
Medical imaging and diagnostics	Optical high-definition imaging and virtual anatomic models Biosensors and markers 4D human charting and virtual reality Screening for diseases
Precision and personalized medicine	Computer-assisted surgery Surgical robots Personalized medicine
Regenerative medicine	Tissue engineering Effective bioartificial pancreas
ORGANISATIONAL AND PROCESS INNOVATIONS	
Novel approaches in healthcare research	Software-based modelling to speed up research Artificial intelligence techniques to speed up research and clinical trials
New ways of delivering healthcare	Telemedicine applications Drone delivery of medications Remote monitoring and portable diagnostics Improved data sharing

Finally, is Scotland creating large healthcare companies for the future?

It appears, under UK industrial policy, that technology leakage to the rest of the world continues through tolerating, even encouraging, the acquisition of key British technology companies by US, Japanese, German, and other expansionist countries. There are many examples. One is the acquisition in 2019 of the start-up Sympromics by Asklepios BioPharmaceutical (AskBio), a North Carolina bio-company. AskBio scoured the world and are buying pockets of skills in various places, including Edinburgh and San Sebastian in Spain, to build a global business. North Carolina has a highly trained bioscience workforce of over 66,000, a community of 735 bioscience companies, 2,400 service providers, and a low cost of doing business. Another example is the successful start-up BioOutsource, from Glasgow, bought by the German and French company Sartorias Stedim to increase its worldwide presence to 20 countries.

What proportion of the 170 start-up companies in Scotland will get the commercial and financial support to become largescale world-size players – Scottish-headquartered companies with access to local risk capital scouring the world of Japan, USA, France and Spain rather than the other way around? The answer lies with both national industrial policy and access to second-stage commercial financing, both pre-requisites for successful long-term wealth creation. Will Scotland's esteemed financial sector, which manages funds of £800 billion, step up?

What have we learned so far from the comparisons?

Cancer is still the most pressing "short term healthcare sprint for Scotland". The failure of the UK to reach a top ten position in health outcomes is mainly a function of underperformance with cancer, with a minor effect from neo-natal care and epilepsy. The latest Quality Watch report of international comparisons describes this issue[13]: *The UK stagnates or significantly lags behind in terms of cancer survival generally, raising concerns about potential delays in diagnosis and timely access to effective treatment for patients. Differences in cancer survival are associated with differences in the readiness of primary care physicians to investigate for cancer... calling for initiatives that would facilitate primary care physicians' ability to investigate and refer to specialists.* Some physicians suggest there may also be a reticence by the public in Scotland to come forward for early investigations.

In contrast, for example, South Korea has created a testing and diagnosis culture. It has a world-renowned system of both publicly and privately funded testing and screening. Every two years its residents receive a battery of tests and a consultation as a free service, a health MoT. They are also encouraged to take further private tests at $600 for the 'basic' level, 'premium' at around $2000, and 'platinum' at over $3000. The health system has created a business out of the service. Foreigners come to South Korea for comprehensive, affordable, and high-quality testing, diagnosis, and treatment. There is no doubt that there is a growing demand in the UK for more screening and early testing. One medical source stated to the authors, "There are downsides to testing. If you test you will always find something! We probably do not test enough, but the USA and some others possibly test too much." The only question is – how can this extra testing be afforded?

Unfortunately, there are no comprehensive studies comparing Scotland internationally to be able to position it independently from the rest of the UK on these comparative outcomes. In April 2014, the Nuffield Trust produced a comparative report, "The four health systems of the UK: How do they compare?"[14]. They concluded that, despite the widely publicised policy differences, there was little evidence that any one country within the UK was moving ahead of the others consistently across the available indicators of performance. As deaths from cardiovascular disease decline thanks to successful treatment regimes, Scotland's top killer is now cancer[15], which therefore needs further attention.

Other "Short Term Healthcare Sprints": The Glasgow Effect, Drugs, Alcohol, Diet and Mental Health

Apparently, five thousand more people die every year in Scotland than should be the case. The reasons are complex but one main contributor is the 'Glasgow Effect,' explained later. The inequalities in deprived areas of the UK, such as Liverpool and Birmingham, with poverty, poor housing and unemployment are documented in reports such as Nuffield's 2020 study. These cities are victims of the so-called Inverse Care Law, i.e. the presence of greater healthcare needs in deprived areas, and yet fewer quality resources available locally. Indeed, deprived areas start with people with more complex health issues who spend a greater proportion of their income on non-health items, have lower self-esteem and self-advocacy, and don't have access to the best professionals. Obesity, heart disease and diabetes, smoking and alcoholism all feature. These diseases can be influenced to a certain extent by lifestyle choices and therefore by better funding for 'public health' in the community. It is more than this, requiring the tackling of body, mind and spirit. For example, adults are twice as likely to have common mental health issues as those in the least deprived areas and have twice the visits to their GPs to deal with anxiety. High quality professionals need to be challenged and incentivised to succeed in these regions.

Scotland has suffered, since the 1990s, from an extreme version of these deprived areas called the 'Glasgow effect,'[16] sometimes known as the 'Glasgow vulnerability.' The excess deaths versus other deprived areas relate mainly to alcohol, drugs, suicide, and violence[17]. Ex-Medical Officer Harry Burns described the special condition as 'a psycho-social problem.' "Where traditional communities lose their traditional cultural anchors, they all find the same things happening – increasing mortality from alcohol, drugs, and violence. The answer is not conventional health promotion. Where you lose a sense of control over your life there is very little incentive to stop smoking or stop drinking or whatever. The answer is to rediscover a sense of purpose and self-esteem." Glasgow has not had the same levels of recovery that some other deprived areas have experienced. Hope and opportunity are still in short supply. Gainful activity is equally scarce for young people. The health issues won't improve until people have the opportunity to create better lives for themselves and build self-esteem: secure jobs; secure homes; stable, loving, and supportive families and communities; and a safe environment. More social cohesion, care, and self-respect; not more hospitals.

The drugs and alcohol factors, although of smaller incidence in the big picture than cancer, are of widespread importance in Scotland. Dundee is currently the drug capital of Scotland and alcohol remains a persistent problem, though to a lesser extent in the last decade. The drug problem is also prevalent in a particular age group, with the median age of death being 42. Again, providing opportunity and gainful activity, and reducing boredom and a sense of hopelessness, play their part in offering solutions.

Lifestyle and diet also have a major impact. Japan's 'secret' is believed to be a combination of diet, lower obesity, a purpose, esteem, and respect for older people beyond retirement. Their free and universal annual medical check-ups and consultations are also renowned. Italy and Spain's success – these are amongst the longest living populations in Europe – is believed to derive from the healthier, Mediterranean diet and the importance of more cohesive inter-generational living and support.

In common with many countries, life expectancy and life-in-good-health are also functions of poverty within a particular nation. In Scotland, the difference between the wealthiest and poorest typically represent a 10-year disparity, a wider gap than for many other countries. This is a blight on society and requires large-scale effective programmes similar to those needed to tackle the Glasgow vulnerability. This is more complex than it seems, however, since there are examples of lower income countries, such as Spain, Portugal, Malta, and Greece having higher life expectancy than Scotland. Poverty is not just a matter of income, but includes the deficiency of support networks, community spirit, friendship, and self-esteem.

"Being unwanted, unloved, uncared for, forgotten by everybody, I think that is a much greater hunger, a much greater poverty than the person who has nothing to eat." – Mother Teresa

Scotland, also in common with other countries, has a growing mental health problem. The issue is complex, with both confusion and controversy over a long period. Pre-WW2, spending was largely on asylums for those classified as insane, involving many controversial and dubious procedures. The 1959 Mental Health Act saw the move away from asylums to care in the community and a significant cut in funding. Confusion reigned over who was responsible for the funding and delivery of community service, and disagreement continued on the root causes of mental illness – behavioural or medical. The preoccupation became focussed on the severely mentally ill and those who presented a risk to society. Then, in the

1970s, the idea of mental health and illness was challenged by the anti-psychiatry movement. The Scottish psychiatrist Lang argued that "Mental illness is a healthy response to a deeply divided world." More recently, mental health is seen to cover a wide range of conditions in a similar way that physical health does. Physical and mental health are integral to each other. Mental illness can be triggered by physical disabilities or illness, genetics, chemical imbalance and circumstantial factors. Mental wellbeing is now recognised as the more appropriate marker for mental health, and is now accepted as having a major impact on society and the economy. The latest shift in recognising this wider definition is certainly a welcome change, but in itself leads to demands for bolder action to tackle the host of old and new challenges that the mental health sector faces on a daily basis.

Fear and anxiety have gripped the young. A recent book by Noreena Hertz, a leading economist[18], has highlighted some of the root causes. A straw poll by the authors of people in their twenties to forties has confirmed many of these trends. A collapse in the belief in opportunity and job security from the financial crisis of 2008, fear of the impending environmental disaster, breakdown of family life and reductions in church-sponsored support, and the growth of social media-induced anxiety and depression are all believed to have some role in this trend. Overall, there is a fear that there is no-one to rely on anymore, resulting in isolation and a feeling of loneliness. Three in five of 18-34-year-olds in the UK feel lonely, often or sometimes. Urbanisation and buzzing city life do not seem to have helped. Counterintuitively, the online world, whilst increasing connectivity, has simply hidden isolation and alienation, and has become a forum for secular sectarianism and cyberbullying. From ancient times the 'wisdom books' have warned us to guard the mind and watch the tongue[19] –

'Do not conform but be transformed by the renewal of your mind that by testing you may discern what is good and what is acceptable'

'Rash words are like swords thrust, but the tongue of the wise bring healing'

– leaving the question, "Can the online world bring us together or does it drive us apart instead?"

A 2020 Netflix documentary titled *The Social Dilemma* hits this issue head on. The early designers of the incredible social media platforms believed they were developing these for social good. Many did not foresee the hijacking of the platforms for the deliberate exploitation of our vulnerabilities for vast profits, control and manipulation, playing with the pain-pleasure response within the body. The documentary goes so far as to claim that 'the very meaning of culture within the social media system of communication is manipulation'. The Fear of Missing Out (FOMO) is encouraged by this platform as is obsession with self-image and the quest for multitudes of affirmations, 'being liked'. In this context it's not surprising that our current mental health programmes are struggling to cope with demand. It is not an exaggeration to classify social media as a new form of addictive drug and the purveyors of it now as unregulated barons. Watch this space – the mental damage caused by social media is only beginning to hit now. Another psycho-social problem not fixable by simply more counsellors or primary care resources.

Surely the revitalisation of vibrant communal hubs, with places for interacting with a diversity of peoples – diverse in age, ethnicity, and outlook – could counter the trend. The reformation of community bonds and the increased participation in the process of decision-making and community building can help ease disenfranchisement and alienation, giving position and respect. Tougher regulation by society is a fair expectation also.

Scotland launched a new ten-year initiative[20] in 2017 to address at least part of the mental health issue, which, according to some studies, affects 1 in 3 of all adults. They have plans for more mental health professionals, training, new parenting programmes, increasing support for new offenders, improved psychological therapy and stronger links of mental health advice for schools, primary care, and police. Self-help digital tools, such as 'CALM' and apps recommended by WHO, will be part of this future initiative. A well designed Cognitive Behavioural Therapy (CBT) app might provide immediate support for some. People will require a variety of approaches in the end.

Will this be enough? Clearly not, other solutions will need to be explored.

Remoteness

Scotland has a particular issue with geographical remoteness and access to excellent health facilities across its Highlands and Islands. This is not currently an issue of hospital coverage. The real issue is the level and quality of investment and operational excellence within the existing structure, and the quality of local primary care leadership and their empowerment within a centrally controlled system. Telemedicine will help to solve some of the issues.

One of the problems for acute care is the lack of a suitable transport network across Scotland. Norway has overcome this to some extent through an air medical service with 12 fixed-wing and 13 helicopters operating from seventeen bases to 11 central hospitals, including high-quality university-based hospitals. Scotland operates two fixed-wing aircraft and four helicopters, surely inadequate for the future to provide world-class cover in sparse regions. The realistic alternative, investment in more remote hospitals, has the risk of reducing remote facilities to the lowest common denominator and increasing the budget substantially. Norway, in its recent attempts to decentralise acute care into the regions, has experienced mixed results at best. Nevertheless, with the melting ice and the need to look North, the future focus will be to invest more in the Shetlands, Orkney, Inverness, and the Western Isles.

Lessons From the recent Pandemic

"No country is fully prepared for epidemics or pandemics. Collectively, international preparedness is weak"

Global Health Security Index Report 2019, pre-Covid-19

Covid-19 has been branded as the invisible war. The deaths in six months are an order of magnitude greater than the total annual deaths of about sixty-five thousand from the major military conflicts in 2019. We had better use this tragedy as a major test run for the future, since pandemics are an inevitable threat from urbanisation and the sheer scale and speed of international travel. What can we learn?

The world was clearly not ready for this pandemic. The UK conducted a simulation study of a major flu-based pandemic in 2016, Exercise Cygnus. The results were never made public. Scotland conducted a table-top exercise, known as Exercise Iris, in 2018, that involved NHS Scotland boards, NHS 24, Health Protection Scotland, and the Scottish Ambulance Service. In 2019, the USA conducted a simulation of a major pandemic that demonstrated the risk of 586,000 deaths and 7.7 million hospitalisations. Yet, the latest crisis has demonstrated that none of these countries was ready for this shock.

The findings from the first ever Global Health Security Index[21] in July 2019 bore no relation whatsoever to the actual experience of 2020. A renowned panel of international experts compared the health security of 195 countries. According to them, the USA, the UK, and the Netherlands were the best prepared in the world. A far cry from the reality of the experience in the first wave of Covid-19. The scores of countries that did well in practice were all over the place in the 2019 rankings, and some of the low-ranked countries turned out to be particularly effective at halting the spread of the virus. South Korea came 9th, Germany 14th, New Zealand 35th, Greece 37th, and the UAE 56th.

Why did the countries ranked top in the assessment perform so badly in practice? The upcoming US Presidential election, Brexit, and the political leadership changes in the UK probably distracted the top politicians of those two nations. Public Health organisations in the UK had been so focussed on chronic diseases and the healthy living agenda – obesity, alcohol, drugs, and sexually transmitted diseases – that they were not fully prepared for this pandemic. They certainly did not have the recent practical experience of handling MERS or SARS, akin to the threat of Covid-19. The authors of the Global Health Security Index maybe underestimated the incentives to look after themselves and their community, especially in countries with more rudimentary hospital systems. Tibetans, for a thousand years right up to the 1950s, practiced cleansing rituals, isolation, and quarantine for returning merchants. Twelve to fourteen days of isolation on returning to the city of Lhasa, with rooms set aside. Kathmandu in Nepal made similar arrangements to prevent medical and spiritual contamination. The widespread use of vaccines and the ability to deal with many pathogens has contributed to the abandonment of these simple policies. The pandemic has shown how hard it is to re-establish these common-sense practices back into society.

Public Health is, rightly or wrongly, the political 'fall guy' in the UK for this pandemic. Yet Public Health objectives are still central to the success of a society. Winslow, the CEO in

1920, certainly had a definition of it that would lead anyone to that conclusion. "Public Health is the science and the art of preventing disease, prolonging life, and promoting physical health and efficiency through organised community efforts for the sanitation of the environment, the control of community infections, the education of the individual in principles of personal hygiene, the organisation of medical and nursing service for the early diagnosis and preventive treatment of disease, and the development of the social machinery which will ensure to every individual in the community a standard of living adequate for the maintenance of health".

This very wide definition is the root of its own problem. It is just too indistinct an objective, after the tangible early role of focussing on encouraging sanitation, vaccinations and child-focussed policies. And it is just too difficult to measure results over a Government term of five years with so many different bodies required to fund and implement recommended actions. It probably doesn't help that Public Health has not yet found a comfortable home within the NHS or Local Government, or society as a whole. The recent dismantling of Public Health England is simply another chapter in this confusion. A review by the Scottish Government identified a number of deficiencies from the original Public Health scheme established in 2004. The recommended changes from 2016 have just been implemented in April 2020. Public Health has never achieved the central position that it required to be a major leading body during an emergency. We also suspect that, in a decade of austerity, it has not been given the funding or "executive teeth" to be able to operate fully.

The assessment in the Global Report could well have missed the human factor altogether. Policy making is one thing, but, as the recent Fraser of Allander report[22] has highlighted, implementation is in the hands of a large number of diverse institutions, companies, and families. Not so easy to impose as fiscal and monetary policy. Not so easy when we have to relearn the collective spirit required to cope with an emergency on a national or world scale. Easy to blame politicians and leaders for our own failings.

Why so slow in testing, including a period when we seemed to abandon the idea? Was it to hide the lack of testing capacity and over-centralisation? Germany seemed much better prepared for testing. Why no "Dunkirk spirit" last seen in the wartime era instead of a central rigid control? Why not an earlier quarantine for overseas arrivals in the UK? How come we sent 16,000 old people back from hospital into care homes before they were tested or before the care home staff were tested and isolated? To save the NHS from appearing to fail? How come we found it much harder than the Swedes to keep the economy going and have similar medical outcomes without having to force a formal lockdown? Are they simply more trusting of their politicians and wiser collectively? Time will tell. Is Japan's system of not shaking hands, of wearing masks, and zealously observing basic hygiene much more effective? Why mandatory face masks so late? The medical advice appeared culpably mixed on that.

One thing is very clear. The care industry has lagged behind best practice operationally, and not just in Britain. It appears that every country in the world was not set up to protect the elderly. The failure to deal with the elderly and care sector could well be one of the main reasons why the report got it wrong.

For exponentially growing diseases, response time is crucial. For example, Taiwan, Hong Kong, Singapore and UAE were quick to test, trace and isolate. Yet some countries dithered and delayed. Lives were lost in the early months through lack of timely decisions and actions: on quarantines; on lockdown, distancing, testing and tracing, and increasing capacity; on getting PPE to the front lines; on flexibility in shifting resources; on mobilising available skills and capacity in military and industry. All of these required slick systems. Because of the remorseless statistics of exponential growth, delay made it exponentially harder to cope.

At an individual level, we can learn how important response time is from the military. When a soldier suffers a traumatic injury or acute infection, the time from event to first medical treatment is usually the single most significant factor in determining the outcome between survival and death, between permanent disablement and living a full life after recovery. This is referred to as the "golden hour," and it is the reason why military forces invest so heavily in moving casualties as fast as possible from battlefield to medical facilities. In the case of Covid-19, the rapid establishment of pop-up ICU facilities was the main action taken to ensure fast response. In one sense, the lockdown is an attempt to buy time to prepare. DARPA, the US Military research agency, created a program to extend the golden hour, not by logistics or battlefield care, but by going after time itself. Molecular biology will be used to slow down the body and extend the interval before it collapses. Essentially, the concept aims to slow life to save life. No doubt other improvements to response time may trickle down from military based research, as they often do. In the case of Covid-19, the wider use of simple oximeters at home under medical supervision, at present under study, could perhaps have led to more golden-hour interventions. It could have identified so-called dangerous "silent hypoxia" earlier.

At a local hospital level, the lack of spare capacity and inflexibility clearly disrupted the ability of the NHS to continue with its full range of services to the public. The intensive care units (ICUs), although stretched to the limit, eventually coped with the needs of Covid-19. However, this was achieved by putting on hold all but emergency services. The inability of the country to deal with non-Covid-19 problems could result in major and long-lasting damage to individuals, society, and the economy. It could, perhaps, be as damaging as the epidemic itself in the long run.

Finally, Covid-19 has demonstrated weaknesses in healthcare resilience and security of medical supply chains and personnel. Security of medical supply chains is now seen as a major national issue, perhaps as important as military security. Scotland will be much more robust once it establishes, where possible, local supply chains and medical onshoring of testing, services, equipment, and workforce.

So, in summary, let's face it, the UK, Scotland included, has come out of this badly internationally, and has a lot to learn from the in-depth reviews in 2021 and beyond. Scotland can certainly learn important lessons on response time, supply of medical equipment, testing, technology, flexibility, workforce adaptability, and medical systems. And it can now also see more clearly that Public Health and the Care Home Sector are not fit for purpose for the next 50 years.

The Authors' Own Experience in the Sector

Although the authors are not medical or healthcare sector experts, they have experienced the sector as practitioners, investors, and patients. Two of the authors were active investors in establishing Greenbrook Healthcare in the primary care sector[23], including urgent care activities under NHS contracts. They have lived and been treated for many years in three different healthcare systems in the world. One has been a trained medical worker in the UK and USA.

The authors have learnt from Greenbrook Healthcare and their own personal experience that the main issue for the NHS is not structural change, which is always a politician's preference to score political points, but simply hands-on operational improvements on the front line. In our view, the less the politicians intervene directly in the running of the NHS, the better. The politicians can set the long-term framework and decide how much to spend. They can delegate to NHS leadership and experts and hold them accountable to scrutiny and audit.

More importantly, quality of care is a direct function of excellence in local leadership and cooperation between medical professionals on the ground. A much greater overall flexibility, a focus on IT (not on grandiose schemes, but on effective use of what's available), administration and clinical quality, and medical accountability at a local level also help. And there are additional benefits from a holistic focus on patient needs, not simply single-minded pursuit of specific targets: care is at its best when the so-called "patient care pathways" are driven from a patient-centric perspective as well as the medic's view. Techniques are available such as the Vanguard Method to capture this thinking and treat the medical processes as a complete system, and eliminate unnecessary steps by automating simple tasks. A key principle is to ensure the service offering is flexible enough to match the variety of demands from patients. The Get it Right First Time Programme is a similar process for improvement by reducing unwarranted variation[24].

The authors have also seen that General Practitioners (GPs) have lost their societal esteem, alongside health visitors, nurses, and other community workers. The prestige goes to the surgeons, the consultants, and the specialists, at the expense of the generalists. Primary care doctors have been encouraged to focus on narrow agendas and cope with a greater demand, rather than 'outside the agenda' services for the community. Furthermore, there are more and more part-time GPs and a breakdown in continuity of the care. GPs have struggled in their role as traditional family doctors; and yet the GP is the one person that can understand their patients within the family unit and their community.

In addition, the entrepreneurial spirit of the 1940s was replaced in the 1990s with more controls and documentation, so that it is not surprising that the ageing primary care medical profession is finding it harder and harder to recruit and retain a new generation of creative and ambitious practitioners. What do we envisage for the future general medical practice? First of all, a reduction of consumer unfriendly waiting rooms, also helpfully reducing nosocomial risk (medical facility acquired infections). The doctor, nurse, psychologist, physiotherapist, and dietician visiting you personally in your own home, not with the old-style physical rounds but by teleconferencing from GP practices, where remote monitoring and simple testing is also conducted. Telemedicine, beginning to be practiced widely, should be used throughout Scotland immediately. We envision a much greater and faster use of personal, remote monitoring, and self-observational devices to improve communication between patients, labs, and medical practitioners. More diagnostics being shifted from Secondary Care to Primary Care. For example, DERM skin cancer diagnosis using AI in GP practices, rather than patients going to hospital to see dermatology specialists. Modern technologies allow accurate testing devices to be manufactured cheaply and in high volume. Why be satisfied with a 24-hour turn-round for testing?

The professionals will thereby have time to do what humans do best – patient observation and intuition to complement technology; interpersonal communication, showing value and respect, personal reassurance, and providing wisdom that follows. The knowledge that someone cares for you is crucial for healing and wellbeing. The GP practices may go a step further than the currently successful GP clustering of 5-8 practices in close geographical proximity. They could provide, if a public/private partnership is acceptable, a wider range of services including physiotherapy, dieticians, life coaching, exercise, massage and beauty therapy, coffee shops, and juice bars, though avoiding the failures of the so-called 'Darzi centres'[25] of a different era. In some cases at least, they would be partly replacing the struggling high street as a place to meet and socialise.

Furthermore, we propose greater emphasis on community care facilities, reducing the misuse of hospitals as surrogate care homes and causing so-called "bed-blocking." Investment in the care of the disabled and elderly, first in the home and then in care homes, is largely missing. The adult care industry employs over 1.7 million[26] and the NHS employs 1.4 million staff in the UK. This labour-intensive sector is ripe for major reform and automation, and there are many ways in which Scotland could become a leader.

One way is to apply the successful adoption of GP clustering into the Care Home sector, to encourage best practice and more sharing of resources. A second, longer term improvement, is the rapid introduction of robotics into the care industry. Robotic Process Automation (RPA) devices tasked to provide basic cleaning and nursing assistance are already emerging. More controversially, Humanoid Nurse Robots (HNRs), which can be caring and more human like, are being conceived for hospital and care home use.

A third solution is to expand the building of senior living communities based on world best practice. The current nursing home model is bluntly not fit for purpose for most of the elderly. An example of the senior living community is the 'Apartments for Life' run by Humanitas[27] in the Netherlands. It is based on four principles: maximum autonomy; family-centred approach; a yes culture; and 'use it or lose it.' And three groups of seniors: 55 and over; those who need some assistance; and those who need regular assistance and medical care. These villages of about 300 homes include community facilities such as supermarkets, cafes, and clubs; and an array of physical and mental activities, combined with the option for life-long learning. An example is U3A, University of the Third Age, designed largely for retired people using the wealth of peer knowledge and experience.

The debate is likely to re-emerge politically on how to deal with the care sector deficiencies. Corbyn, pre Covid-19, proposed a National Care System and Theresa May was considering tax proposals instead. From our perspective the main point is not which political system to adopt. More importantly, what investment in medical technology and best practice should we make both within the home and in care homes?

> *"Hospitals are only an intermediate stage of civilisation, never intended … to take the whole sick population. May we hope that the day will come … when every poor, sick person will have the opportunity of a share in a district nurse at home." – Florence Nightingale, 1820-1910*

What are the Big, Long Term Opportunities for Scotland?

First and foremost, can Scotland succeed in this sector at all? The simple answer is yes. This is a large, high-growth, high-profit sector of the world economy. It's also clear, from even a superficial assessment, that life sciences and healthcare are indeed Scottish strengths. Don't let anyone tell you otherwise. Those who doubt it must only rarely have experienced unequal and very expensive healthcare systems such as the USA's, or inadequate systems in the developing world. In Michael Porter's famous Harvard Business School book, *The Competitiveness of Nations*, he identifies attractive sectors as having three characteristics: long-term demographics and sustained growth; positions of competitive advantage; and structures with good investment returns, both financial and social. Life sciences and healthcare have all three characteristics for Scotland.

But there is another good reason why Scotland should succeed in this sector. Scotland has very few opportunities for sustained economic growth. If it fails, it could be trapped by the insatiable medical inflation that continues to consume the national budget of every nation on this planet. Taking advantage of the melting ice, reversing the wet desert, building a renewable energy sector and investing in marine and financial services are all great opportunities. But the vision of a healthy, wealthy, and wise Scotland will be jeopardised if wealth from these opportunities is simply consumed by the ageing population and increased needs of its own people.

Having established that this is both an attractive and a necessary sector for Scotland to invest in, now is the time to lay out what should be the priorities for the future. Here is our answer: the healthcare waves we should be surfing for the next fifty years.

Surf the Brain Wave

"It is time to start anew. More than a century after neuropathologist Alois Alzheimer gave the first scientific talk describing the disease that bears his name today, we have no good treatments for this thief of minds, and we certainly have no cure."

Josh Fischman, Senior Editor of Scientific America

The first priority is to participate as a leader in the emerging area of brain healthcare and sciences. Fortunately, Scotland has already started to surf this (brain) wave. Brain Health Scotland, the Scottish Dementia Research Consortium, the Scottish Dementia Working

Group, the National Dementia Carers Action Network are all working towards a leading position in this world trend. Some strong leaders, internationally recognised, are driving the initiatives with solid political backing. Examples include Sir Adrian Bird, from Edinburgh University, winning the largest world prize for neuroscience, awarded from Denmark; and Professor Craig Ritchie, National Director of Brain Health Scotland, triggering a national initiative to capture the high ground with an attitude that brain health starts at an early age, and is not just an old persons' problem. For example it will include mental health initiatives to overcome the growing mental wellbeing challenges that the younger generations face. At the same time it requires older people to remain socially active, maintain exercise and good nutrition, and face new challenges and activities well beyond retirement.

Admittedly, heart medicine has not yet fully had its day, but large breakthroughs in cardiovascular research have taken place since the first heart transplant 43 years ago. Cardiovascular disease, still a significant killer, is on its way down the pecking order. Triple heart bypasses, heart transplants, stents, and statins have already become household words. AI, psychology, computer science, and medical science are all homing in on the next big leap, the understanding of the brain. The jargon you had better become familiar with includes terms such as cognitive science, systems neuroscience, cellular and molecular neuroscience, and computational medicine. Get used to the image of the brain being at the centre of healthcare, where the symbol of the heart used to be – not just hearing about heart attacks or strokes, but 'brain attacks.' And get used to the fact that this is not just about dementia and Alzheimer's as the population ages further and other health conditions are improved, but also about the effects of brain health more widely.

Revamp Primary Care

Primary care has become a second fiddle in the orchestra. The role of the general practitioner and nurse in the community has been relegated to a somewhat secondary place. We have a few suggestions that will help restore them to a leading position: first of all, the rapid automation of administrative tasks is urgently required to release medical staff and allow them to develop stronger relationships with individuals, their families, and the community. The trust and knowledge gained will enhance their role to become greater pillars of support. Secondly, it's time to invest in new patient/professional interfaces from telemedicine, smart diagnosis, and reductions in traditional waiting rooms – not least to keep up with a younger generation who rely on technology as simply an extension of their own persona. Thirdly, we can learn more from successful urgent care centres and super-centres – psychologists, physiotherapists, dieticians. We recommend broader targets and greater resources to tackle psychological, nutritional, and mental health. Mental health, a very complex societal issue, does require lateral thinking to generate a range of ad-hoc solutions, supported by self-help apps, helpline access, and more listening and active counsellors. Finally, technologies, such as AR and VR, will emerge to service certain aspects of physical and mental health as the population ages, the demands grow, and the available working population shrinks.

Invest more substantially in Public Health

In parallel to the revamping of primary care, a greater investment in Public Health is called for, despite its recent experience as the fall guy. The establishment of Public Health as the 'Champion of the People' with greater positional authority is a priority – an institution fighting against disease, both invisible and visible. And not with more advertising campaigns alone. There have been plenty of those, including the latest on obesity. We recommend more societal clout. Dare we say it, greater legislation and more concerted efforts to overcome the minority vested interests in society. The war on smoking involved legislation, bans on advertising, pricing, and other substantial action to go along with education campaigns. Car safety required the mandatory use of seat belts. Alcohol is being tackled with taxation and pricing legislation to influence behaviour. Tackling obesity and exercise requires equal levels of strength and action. In common with primary care, leadership, decision-making authority and accountability in Public Health are essential.

We see a greater role for Public Health in tackling the negative impact of social media on the wellbeing of the nation. Obsession with self-image, bullying, personal abuse, and hate crimes are coming off the streets and are expected to continue to grow rapidly online. It's not just viruses that are invisible, online personal attacks are equally so.

The country would benefit from a long-term shift in culture. Easy to say, but hard to achieve. Encouraging more individual responsibility for our own health, and understanding better the basic benefits of hygiene, sanitation and ventilation in the home, nutrition, exercise, and the advantages of spending time outdoors. One subtle condition for this to work is a non-judgemental society and an increase in the spirit of encouragement. For example, many unfit or obese people do not go to gyms or exercise because they feel they will be judged as soon as they are seen.

Perhaps we could even create some more formal, supportive institution – a healthcare equivalent to the military's Territorial Army. Or a form of domestic Peace Corps for our own communities. "Serve where you are needed most." A form of community service and self-discipline that could include healthcare support training and fitness encouragement. This would certainly have been a helpful voluntary force during the recent pandemic.

Develop Leadership in the Care Sector

A number of countries have already identified the potential from the growth of the so-called 'Silver Economy' – goods and services aimed at people over the age of fifty. We recommend that Scotland take three actions relevant for healthcare within this growing marketplace.

The first is simply to encourage the establishment of clusters of care homes to share best practice and to share resources within the cluster. The second is to be an early adopter of new smart home technologies for the elderly and for the automation of care homes. Robots can be used for many tasks: talking companions, instructor and exercise companions, and care and cleaning. They are improving all the time, able increasingly to respond to emotions. They are dependable, undemanding, responsive day and night. Super-Alexas, named after the Library of Alexandria. ELLI-Q, another companion device to keep older adults sharp, connected and engaged, developed by the Israelis, named after the Norse for old age – Elli – and found to be very helpful for those in isolation during Covid-19. Through its research in robotics, AI, and the related research on the brain, automation in care homes could be a focal point for the future of Scotland.

The third is to encourage the widespread expansion of 'silver villages' for over 55 year olds and retired individuals with activities, medical facilities, and life learning programmes. We would recommend these villages to be built using the wood-based technologies and renewable energy resources described in other chapters, with local primary care supercentres within easy reach.

Create Larger Scottish-based Healthcare Companies

A change in industrial policy is required if this has any hope of success. The French have a much better system of defending successful start-ups and small, embryonic companies from being swallowed up by well-funded American, Japanese, Chinese, and other European companies. This applies to other sectors of the economy also and is discussed in other chapters of this book. But the Scottish medical sector is particularly vulnerable to an international raid right now because it has been so active with University-based start-ups and business parks over the last 10 years that it is producing rich pickings.

Further actions are recommended. Link university hospitals, research centres, start-ups, and global companies even more strongly. Balance increased operational autonomy, essential for resilience, with increased international collaboration, crucial to maintaining expertise and getting the best value from R&D expenditure. Insource selected strategic medical supplies as part of a shift in national industrial policy, and increase cooperation with similar minded countries. Further invest funds from the Edinburgh-based financial services industry, the Scottish Investment Bank, and the Scottish Government. All of this will be required to achieve this noble aim.

In conclusion...

Finally, we hear you say, healthcare leadership is unachievable without extra funding. We agree. Our own guestimate is that a further 1-2% of GDP – around 600 pounds per person in Scotland – is required within a decade to support this programme, based on international benchmarks. An increase of at least 0.2% of GDP in medical equipment spending. A doubling of medical research, in common with other sectors of the economy, and a tripling of development spending will be fundamental. Extra money for Primary Care and Public Health should be provided, not least for the short-term healthcare sprints, without compromising the needs and excellence of the secondary care sector.

References for Chapter 5

[1] Measuring performance on the Healthcare Access and Quality Index for 195 countries and territories and selected subnational locations: a systematic analysis from the Global Burden of Disease Study 2016. The Lancet

[2] International Comparisons of Healthcare Quality. Quality Watch, 2015

[3] How Good is the NHS? Nuffield Trust 2018

[4] Commonwealth Fund. Mirror, Mirror 2017- International Comparison, July 2017

[5] Health at a Glance, 2019 OECD INDICATORS

[6] Learning from Scotland's NHS, Nuffield Trust, July 2017

[7] Kraindler, Gershlick. International Comparisons of Capital in Health Care, October 2019

[8] World University Ranking 2020, Times Higher Education

[9] QS World University Ranking Medical Schools, 2020

[10] QS Top Nursing Schools, 2019

[11] GVA Figure provided by Fraser of Allander Institute, 2019: "The_economic_contribution_of_the_pharmaceutical_industry_in_Scotland"

[12] Abstracted from GLOBAL INNOVATION INDEX 2019 Creating Healthy Lives—The Future of Medical Innovation
Sources: GII 2019 chapters, in particular Collins, 2010; Collins, 2019. Also, Kraft, 2019; Nature, 2018; Nature, 2019; Frost & Sullivan, 2018; Frost & Sullivan, 2019; European Commission, 2007; Medical Futurist, 2017; Mesko, 2018.

[13] Focus on: International Comparison of Healthcare Outcomes, July 2015 Quality Watch, Nuffield Trust

[14] The Four Health Systems of the United Kingdom. How do they Compare? Nuffield Trust and Health Foundation, April 2014

[15] National records of Scotland. Scotland's Population – the registrar general's annual review of demographic trends - 2018.

[16] Ellie Harrison, The Glasgow Effect, Luath 2019

[17] Walsh, McCartney, Collins, Taulbut, Batty. History, Politics and Vulnerability: Explaining Excess Mortality in Scotland and Glasgow, May 2018

[18] The lonely Century: Coming together in a world that is pulling apart, Noreena Hertz, 2020

[19] Romans 12 v 2, Proverbs 12 v 15

[20] Mental Health Strategy 2017-2027 Scottish Government

[21] https://www.ghsindex.org

[22] https://fraserofallander.org/fai-publications/what-can-we-learn-from-previous-pandemics-and-from-the-response-to-covid-19-so-far/

[23] Primary Care Services provide the first point of contact, acting as the 'front door' of the NHS. Includes general practice, community pharmacy, dental, and optometry (eye health) services.

[24] Get It Right First Time (GIRFT). National programme designed to improve medical care within the NHS.

[25] Uncorrected transcript of oral evidence to the House of Commons Health Select Committee. Hansard. 17 July 2008.

[26] NHS Workforce January 2020 and NHS Scotland, Scotland's Health on the Web.

[27] Centre for Public Impact, Apartments for Life in the Netherlands, August 2018

Chapter 6

Doubling R & Tripling D

"Innovation is one percent inspiration and ninety-nine percent perspiration"

Commonly attributed to Thomas Edison

Scotland can be a successful innovative nation again. But to do that, it needs to double its research and triple its development spending – R2D3! To give Scotland the most benefit, this investment must go hand in hand with re-vitalising the engineering and tech business ecosystems – home-grown businesses big and small that can create wealth and jobs in Scotland by producing world-beating products and services, and successfully delivering big complex projects. The increased research and development money is best directed towards Scotland's existing strengths – medical, marine, renewable energy and financial services – and the new opportunities in AI, 21st-century manufacturing, and next generation engineered timber products and structures.

The funding could come from re-examined defence policy, or from a return to Keynesian economics in a low inflation environment – or by offering sustainable long-term investment returns to Norway's €1trn Sovereign Wealth Fund!

"It's the Economy Stupid"

'One person in your waiting room.'

John clicked on admit. Simon's face appeared on his Zoom call. His lips moved, but John heard nothing. "It might help if you were to unmute your microphone!"

Simon smiled ruefully. "Always forgetting".

"Anyway, how are you doing, John? Are you still at home, or are you jetting all over the place again now the lockdown's over? Where are you today? The picture behind you looks distinctly un-British."

"Emirati art. Riyadh on Saturday. Back home in Abu Dhabi next week if plans don't change. Running around like crazy to get our Middle East project going again after the lockdown."

Simon smiled. "Glad you still have time to talk to a home body like me then. The furthest I got to on business was London and Kirkwall. You know, the best thing about lockdown was discovering just how much of our work we could do by video conference. Right now I feel I never want to see the inside of an aeroplane again!

"Maybe it's time to retire. My Stanford University classmates think I'm crazy still working. All right for them. They made fortunes in the financial markets of New York and London in the nineties. Us engineers, just toil and trouble!"

"Simon, I wouldn't miss our discussions for the world. Keep me sane. Keep me connected to the homeland while I gallivant around the world."

"So, what did you make of our reading list this time?" asked Simon. "A bit different from the stuff Angela's book group has been reading."

They had set themselves, pre Covid-19, the mammoth task of reading Gordon Brown's book *My Scotland, Our Britain*[1], and the Scottish Growth Commission Report[2], as well as *Arguing for Independence* by the late Stephen Maxwell[3].

"A seriously heavy read this time," commented John, "But I was so glad that you suggested it. I was so tired of hearing about the virus and its disastrous effect on the economy. It's good to be reminded of the big long-term issues for Scotland, the things people were talking about before the virus clobbered us. Glad we gave ourselves a few weeks though. Tough reading!"

"Yes, me too. It's surprising how some of the arguments of 2014 have now been turned completely on their head," mused Simon. "Covid-19 and oil prices for a start. Not to mention the notion that staying in the UK was any sort of safe 'status quo.' Whatever happened to 'Vote no to keep Scotland in the EU?' Whatever happened to 'Strong and stable?' Just shows you have to look at the future of a country in the long run, not a politicians' five years."

"Yes, *events young man, events*. But what did you think of Gordon Brown's assessment of the Scottish Economy five years ago?" asked John, "I see he's back on the scene promoting global cooperation."

"I thought he laid out the problems for the Scottish economy pretty well. Long-term decline of manufacturing. Poor applied research spending even in UK terms, 0.6% of GDP versus 1.0 % for the UK as a whole. Decline of oil wealth. Low business birth rate – Scotland only has five or six percent of UK start-ups. Not so well positioned for Asia. Seventy percent of exports tied to England. More reliant on exports than some other small countries…"

Simon tailed off. John continued the tale of woe. "… and of course, he's very worried about Financial Services. 8-9% of the Scottish Economy, and with the risk of independence, they would all leave for bigger countries with a more secure currency."

"That's only a problem if financial services benefit the economy in the first place," countered Simon. "I read a report[4] that said financial services COST Britain two years' GDP in the last twenty – destroyed ten percent of the economy's value – by misallocating resources, and by extracting profits instead of reinvesting them."

"All those maths and engineering and science graduates going into finance, instead of adding value to the real economy through industry and teaching and research. And that's his next point. He says that Scotland's universities don't have enough scale and profile to attract the funding for the next generation of ideas and businesses." John paused, and summed up: "So, all in all, he was pretty miserable. Lots of problems, not a lot of opportunities."

"Yes. but this is where I really don't get it. He uses that as an argument to stay in the Union – we are too small and too plugged-in economically to survive on our own. Yet it's within the Union that this miserable state of affairs has occurred," replied Simon. "What's going to change?"

"But that's his point. He thinks somehow that changing to a Federal model within the Union will magically trigger the UK to solve these problems – keeping our universities world class, investing in R&D, focusing on knowledge services. I really wish I could believe that would do it. I just don't see how rearranging the constitutional deck chairs would make any difference. More like we need major reinvestment."

Sensing John was about to go off on an extended rant, Simon jumped in quickly. "Where's that going to come from, then?"

"Not exactly clear. I guess higher taxes under the federal model he's promoting," speculated John. "Maybe we should ask him?"

"But that's the very criticism that Labour and the Tories are making against the SNP. Tax raising party!" interjected Simon.

"Well, I guess as a former Chancellor of the Exchequer and Prime Minister, he might know a few things. He pretty much rescued the world economy in the 2009 financial crisis, after all!"

"But everything's changed in the last few months. Even neoliberal economists are now embracing Keynesianism. Chancellors found the magic money tree after all. A sensible government would launch a massive stimulus package to shift as fast as possible to zero carbon, circular economy, warm affordable homes for all, regenerative agriculture, all those good things."

Simon responded, somewhat scathingly. "Show me a sensible government!"

They agreed Gordon Brown made some odd choices in the countries he compared Scotland with. He claimed Iceland and Ireland coming a cropper in the 2007-8 financial crisis proved the awful fate that would undoubtedly befall an independent Scotland. He ignored the successful Scandinavian countries; he ignored Iceland's and Ireland's naivety launching into financial services without understanding the risks. And, though he couldn't have known when he wrote the book, his argument is now undermined by both countries' rapid and successful recovery. This, claimed John, proved the point made by the Growth Commission that small, advanced countries can respond to economic shocks more quickly and effectively than large ones.

Simon suggested the Growth Commission contradicted itself: on the one hand asserting that Scotland, if independent, must not follow the UK's austerity policies; yet on the other, putting a high priority on fiscal prudence and near-balanced budgets. "But maybe the deficit isn't as big a problem as we all think. As long as interest rates and inflation stay low, you can safely issue stimulus funds to create new jobs. The important thing is to look to the future – long-term sustainable investments in new industries and infrastructure, not propping up over-paid jobs in dying industries."

"Printing money you mean?"

"Not really; just old-fashioned Keynesianism, like in the 1930s and 40s. Investing in the future instead of subsidising the past. Though you probably need your own currency to do it successfully."

"OK Simon, so if we're not convinced about Brown's proposals, what did you think of the Fraser of Allander Report[5] you sent me a few weeks ago? I haven't had a chance to absorb it properly yet."

"Thought that was sensible, much more forward looking. A bit short on tangible suggestions. But addresses many of the underlying problems. Their main conclusions – invest in infrastructure, focus on knowledge-based industries, fix the start-up deficiencies, and scale up."

"They mention the popular Fintech, digital skills, Cyber-security, and increasing R&D within businesses. Quite a lot about productivity, though a bit thin on how to do it. But there's one thing they said that I thought was really key – the importance of collaboration to build scale."

"That fits with the big theme in the report that I'm very keen on. How to ramp up the export base. I have always believed that Scotland could do with a heavy dose of American brashness and commercial nous. Without the arrogance. Maybe that's impossible. No doubt Scottish businesses could invest much more in their commercial skills. A bit too meritocratic and introverted for my liking. My New York based training with Yul Brinner – remember him, the actor in *The King and I* – well, he was one of the instructors on the training course. It was a real shock. They tried to knock my Scottish modesty out of me. My mother would have been horrified!"

"Anyway," concluded John, "Sounds like you found that a good read."

"It was, but it left me craving for more detail and concrete ideas."

"So, what did you make of the book by... oh, that SNP chap who died not long ago?"

"You mean Stephen Maxwell's *Arguing for Independence*? Different book altogether," said Simon. "Logical, well rounded arguments; short on economic facts, more emotional. Feels very dated already. Lots about politics; not much about how to attract people back to build a prosperous future. Lots about the need for new social policies; not much about creating the wealth to pay for them."

"All comes back to money in the end, doesn't it?" said John.

"Unless you're a rabid Green!" Said Simon. "I don't know if they all think that way, but the Greens we know just want to crash the economy. Stop using fossil fuels, just like that. 'Degrowth,' they call it. I even hear there's a Scottish Degrowth Commission!"

"I certainly don't buy the degrowth stories I'm hearing," observed John. "The virus cut pollution and oil consumption. But look at the cost to the economy. Is that what they want? I can't see how the Glasgow poor will vote for that... maybe the middle class and rural dropouts."

"It's just crazy," said Simon. "We got to the Moon in eight years. The Manhattan project built the atomic bomb in four years. Look at how quickly planes evolved: the Wright brothers flew 400 yards in 1903, Alcock and Brown flew across the Atlantic in 1919. Incredible achievements. If we can just formulate this climate problem properly and tackle it head on, on a war footing, we must be able to improve lives, not wreck them.

"People keep saying 'where's the money going to come from?' Scotland's Financial Services sector has £800 billion under management[6]. That's five times Scotland's GDP. Are they managing that money on behalf of Scotland, or just extracting it from us? Investing in new high-tech zero carbon industries would create a better future for the whole nation, secure our future for a century[7]. Surely that's an investable proposition?"

Simon paused for effect before delivering his coup de grace.

"So why do we keep talking about needing foreign money to invest in our future? Why can't our financial services industries step up to the plate?"

"That reminds me," interjected John, "Have you seen that book by Business for Scotland, *Scotland the Brief?*"

"No I haven't. Great title. How about the content?", replied Simon.

"Yes, excellent summary on some of Scotland's existing successes, and how well off we are for natural resources. Really good baseline. An antidote to Gordon Brown's more downbeat assessment. Needs a sequel to look into the future more. Definitely worth a read though."

They were still hard at it when Angela interrupted them. "Hello John, lovely to see you. You look well! Sorry to interrupt, I've got to drag Simon away – grandson duty! Christine's car is outside, Finn will be at the door in a minute, Adam is desperately hungry! Give my love to Evelyn. Byeee!"

Just before Angela stopped them, John went off on another whimsical rant. "Did I ever tell you, I met Lord Hanson once in the 1980s? He told me privately that he was very angry at America getting all our smart technology in return for their support in the War. He blamed Churchill for handing them all our best bits at far too cheap a price. Hanson wanted to get his own back by buying up as much of America as possible, cheaply, when the US was struggling in the early 1980s. Especially in basic industries. He was quite successful for a while as it turned out."

"The stats are certainly quite striking. America's GDP increased by 300% during World War 2. The major European powers' fell by 70%," interjected Simon.

"Yes, the economic price of war," added John. "So, does that make two of the so-called greats, Churchill and Thatcher, actually leaving us in worse shape? Churchill gave away great secrets and wealth and took on a crippling dollar debt, all in four years. Thatcher destroyed large chunks of our industrial base and didn't rebuild anything, and she was in power for ten years."

"Maybe a third in the making! The current Prime Minister and his backers completing what Churchill and the Lady started. Making us even more dependent on the USA. Reverse colonisation!" mused Simon.

It's the Economy Stupid – yes, really!

Scotland, like the rest of the world, is still reeling from the impact of the Coronavirus pandemic. But our fundamental structural problems run much deeper.

Shipbuilding, mining, car manufacturing and many other industries were wiped out in the 1980s and 1990s, along with the skilled and well-paid jobs they created. And this is without mentioning the previous devastation from the second world war and its abrupt end with a crushing debt, which created its own economic decline and a culture of chronic under-investment. Silicon Glen, the effort to attract foreign electronics companies from Japan and Silicon Valley to invest in Central Scotland, had mixed results at best: a short-term boost, but too many assembly plants and not enough leading-edge R&D, making the project unsustainable in the long term. Nor have we used the 30-year oil boom to create successful world-scale companies headquartered locally, with one or two exceptions.

Scotland was naïve in thinking it could replicate Silicon Valley. California's success didn't come from a bunch of entrepreneurs in a free market, riding a consumer electronics trend. It grew out of decades of superlative and heavily funded work at two major research universities, UC Berkeley and Stanford, and out of a government-sponsored Space Programme.

The combined wealth and knowledge of the State of California, the Federal Government, and these highly funded Universities boasting large numbers of Nobel prize winners, created a fertile breeding ground for start-ups. In the 1970s, Apple's founders Steve Wozniak and Steve Jobs built computers for hobbyists using silicon chips developed with billions of government dollars. SUN Microsystems – SUN stands for Stanford University Networks – was launched out of Stanford in the 1980s. SUN's founder wrote a cheque for $100,000 to form Google with two Stanford Students; and so the story goes on!

Mariana Mazzucato's book *The Entrepreneurial State*[8] (published in 2013) came too late to influence the current generation of UK politicians and economists. She shows that the State has a major role in shaping economies, providing the groundwork for success, and funding big long-term risky enterprises that the private sector would never contemplate.

The reliance on Financial Services in London and Scotland has sucked us dry of new ideas elsewhere in the economy.

This has to change.

There is a strong long-run relationship between key indicators of innovation (including patents) and economic growth. With its R&D spend less than half of Finland's and Sweden's, and near the bottom of the rich world league table for R&D and patents, it's not surprising that Scotland is falling way behind.

The free market thinking of recent times has turned out to be a false doctrine. It was not the free market but the Marshall Plan, a massive government-led Keynesian stimulus, that rebuilt Europe after the devastation of the second world war. The free market winners have been the new low-cost economies of the East. Not a bad thing, it has pulled billions out of poverty, but it's not a panacea. In the West, hedge fund bosses and house owners did well; others lost out.

If Scotland is serious about having a Silicon Valley equivalent, rather than competing with Ireland as a non-research, low tax, trading nation like Ireland, it will need to double, perhaps triple, its investment in research & development. We require a major boost for universities, and perhaps a fundamental restructuring of the sector. But more importantly, we could make it easier and faster for promising innovations to cross the 'valley of death' from applied research to product and market development. All this to emulate the more successful economies of Sweden, Finland and Denmark. The models for Scotland's future success are there. It's a matter of adapting them to our opportunities and circumstances, not reinventing them.

Job creation in the new world will be about the 'knowledge economy' – software, IT, AI and informatics, life sciences, and smart integration across any and all of these rapidly evolving fields. Manufacturing jobs will only come back if we use these new technologies in the approach the Germans call "Industrie 4.0," to improve productivity, quality, whole-life cost, environmental footprint, and responsiveness to customers' needs, as import substitution is seen as increasingly desirable for environmental and economic reasons. Export business will follow if and when, like Germany and Sweden, we become best in the world at what we do. Along with the trends and opportunities addressed in chapters two to five (looking north, reforestation, renewables, and healthcare), we believe that this future lies in innovation in three to four more sectors of the economy, that is, financial services, AI and digital technology, and maritime industries. At the same time, we echo the call for 'novelty is not enough,' and ask how to increase the value to Scotland of Scotland's potential for innovation.

Financial Services

Innovation and a Lower Cost Skill Base

Financial Services is a growth industry worldwide and one of Scotland's strengths.

Financial services already form a key part of the Scottish economy: almost 6% of employment and about 9% of GDP (versus UK 11%). Scotland's financial sector employs[9] 86,000 directly, of whom more than half (44,000) work in banking. Another 75,000 work in professional services firms whose success is tied closely to the financial sector. It has world-class capabilities in banking, investment management and asset servicing, and insurance and pensions. Its combination of high skills and lower cost than most European financial hubs places it excellently for the future.

For a small country, we're a big player. The Global Financial Centres Index (GFCI) ranks Edinburgh 17th in the world and number six in Europe, ahead of Luxembourg, and close behind Paris, Zurich and Frankfurt[10]. If Edinburgh and Glasgow were thought of together, their combined ranking would be even higher.

How much of this success is home-grown, and how much depends on being part of the UK? And indeed, how much depended on being part of the EU?

Some of Scotland's success as a financial centre is down to its natural advantages, its skilled and well-educated workforce, its long history, and its reputation for financial rectitude.

This reputation was severely dented by the series of disasters that afflicted the Royal Bank of Scotland (RBS) before, during, and after the financial crisis of 2007-8. Over-ambitious expansion was followed by a catastrophic collapse when the world financial system crashed in 2007. The Bank only survived because of a massive taxpayer bail-out, and it is still 62% owned by the UK Government. RBS's reputation suffered further from the revelations of a parliamentary enquiry on the treatment of small businesses by the bank's restructuring unit[11]. RBS is still a big world player, but it has slipped from its peak in 2007 to number six in the world. Its staff numbers shrank by two-thirds between 2007 and 2019, from 226,000 to 77,000. It still employs 11,000 in Scotland, a quarter of our banking workforce, but RBS is now in a real sense a UK-owned international banking group, rather than a Scottish one. Likewise, the Bank of Scotland, whose Scottish presence has been hollowed out as a result of its merger with Halifax and the TSB, can hardly be considered quintessentially Scottish.

If the world – and notably Iceland – learned one thing from the financial crisis of 2007-2008, it is that big international banks are only viable if they have the backing of big countries' governments. The pandemic has reinforced that view. A small country simply cannot afford the risk of being home to big international private-sector banks. Be home to its infrastructure and back office operations: most certainly. Underwrite its mistakes and misfortunes and risky adventures in third countries: most certainly not.

One thing is absolutely clear: the headquarters of RBS would move to London if Scotland became independent, taking with it at least 1000 Scottish jobs. That may happen even under a more radical federal system. Advocates of independence must face the fact that unless Scotland remains part of a larger entity, those thousand jobs are gone. Scotland cannot play host to the headquarters of world-scale financial companies needing world-scale government financial backing. This is not a matter of pride. It's plain common sense.

The good news is, the health of Scotland's financial sector no longer depends just on the large banks. Numerous specialist businesses large and small thrive in our financial ecosystem. If Scotland were to return to the EU, or stay closely tied to it, we could compete for European business on a much larger scale. Only Dublin would share our attractiveness for foreign investments as an English-speaking location with access to the EU single market.

(But we are falling into the trap that we warned our readers to avoid. Focus on the fundamental market opportunities, don't get distracted by the politics.)

There are growing opportunities for specialised financial services roles relating to Scotland's own industrial policies, to finance renewables, emerging Arctic projects, reforestation, life sciences, innovative housing, future technologies such as AI, and closer links with the financial sectors of its Nordic neighbours.

Let's call a spade a spade: we want the Scottish financial sector to focus on sustainable investments in Scotland's real economy of jobs and resources, rather than focussing on the pure financial markets that have grown at the expense of the real economy in the last two decades.

AI and Digital Industries

The knowledge economy and the tech ecosystem

Traditional Information and Computing Technology, as well as the newer Artificial Intelligence and Software sectors, are blurring as we speak. The fourth Industrial Revolution is well underway, and Scotland should focus on its sectoral strengths to benefit from this new revolution. One such example is transdisciplinary informatics, combining medical, psychological, computer, and digital thinking into new disciplines.

The obvious places for Scotland to focus on are MediTech, Fintech, and Gaming, where the country has sectoral strength already; on highly customised specialist manufacture, using the latest distributed manufacturing techniques to produce local products for local markets; and on adding value to the marine and renewables industries, transport, logistics, and energy distribution with smart data analysis and dynamic control.

The key, as found in the NewTech centre around Old Street in London, is to encourage cheap, vibrant hubs where lifestyle seeking millennial AI and Software people can live, breathe, and create new products. We don't need the regimented business parks in the best parts of town or far out in the country, with beautifully manicured avenues and expensive high-quality offices. What we need is neighbourhoods studded with coffee bars, cheap food, and affordable accommodation.

Getting our Tech Ecosystem past the tipping point

One of the authors recalls: 'I remember in the mid '90s sitting in a packed lecture hall at the Heriot Watt, watching half a dozen young folk getting a prestigious prize for an exciting new high-tech product. The money spent on feeding the expensively suited audience would probably have moved the start-up business on a stage in their commercialisation. But I don't think any of the smartly dressed well-paid audience could actually help the company work out what to do next. I spent some time talking to them afterwards, as part of my company's civil diversification efforts, but we couldn't find a fit between our business model and theirs.'

Mark Logan is different from those hundreds of besuited folk in that audience fifteen years ago. He's been there, done that. and helped grow a native Scottish software business (Skyscanner) to 'unicorn' status – a business worth over a billion pounds. Now it's owned by China.

Why do so few of Scotland's start-ups get to the point of scaling up to serious businesses generating substantial revenue and employment? And why do so many of those that do, gradually loosen their ties with Scotland?

Mark Logan's Scottish Technology Ecosystem Review, released by the Scottish Government on 25 August 2020, sets out to answer these questions. The answers will be exciting to many, because we can do so much better. It will be deeply uncomfortable to some, because, according to his review, current approaches to supporting start-ups are not merely not helping them, but are often actively impeding.

The report is a blueprint for how to make Scotland's tech start-up scene wealth-generating, job-creating and self-sustaining. Silicon Valley and London have crossed a tipping point where their high-tech scenes are self-sustaining, employees can move to another local company if their venture fails or their job doesn't work out, investors are making enough money they can plough their profits into more growing companies, and the area becomes a worldwide magnet for talent. This means, crucially, that companies can scale up without moving away. Scotland has not reached that tipping point. Without that scale, almost every successful start-up either sells out or moves away, so that their jobs and profits and taxes end up elsewhere. And not enough are successful - too many stick at 30-50 employees and can't make the transition from start-up to rapid – or indeed any – growth.

How to do differently? For the details, read the report rather than have us repeat its recommendations. We simply highlight the essence of what is required: only world-class skills are good enough in software, business start-ups, and the leadership and management challenges of starting up rapidly; a talent pipeline, including, but well beyond education, into experience; success measured not at the individual business level, but with an eye to its contribution to the whole tech community; a virtual and real, unglamorous infrastructure that supports start-ups; and a key learning that local optimisation is the enemy of global optimisation. Individuals, towns, and institutions compete against each other instead of uniting to make Scotland a world player. The high cost of commuting between Edinburgh and Glasgow halves the available labour pool in both cities and reduces the network effect by even more. This point is addressed in our next chapter with the belief that Scotland needs to act as a medium-sized 'Virtual City' rather than a fragmented set of small, competing entities scattered throughout the country.

With Logan's blueprint, each player can see how they fit (or not) into the whole picture, and how they contribute (or not) to the success of the whole. There's a long way to go – this is about a blueprint for a new way of growing serious job-creating businesses in Scotland. It's focused on the 'Tech' (software) sector, but the general principles are applicable across the whole of the knowledge economy – complex product engineering, high-tech manufacture, integrated infrastructure, renewables, and the zero-carbon transition. Wouldn't it be nice if instead of tearing lumps out of each other, the different political parties were competing to say how they will deliver on this blueprint?

Scotland: six times more sea than land

A marine industrial policy

Scotland has a longer coastline than China. Scotland's marine EEZ (Exclusive Economic Zone) is nearly half a million square kilometres, six times the area of our land. We have a large fraction of Europe's fish stocks, and a thriving (though now mainly foreign-owned) fish farming industry. At any one time over 30,000 oil workers live in our marine offshore village. We have increasing interests in wave and tidal energy and offshore wind power for the future. Our spent oil and gas reservoirs make up a large fraction of Europe's Carbon Capture and Storage (CCS) potential. We have the largest natural deep-water port in Europe, Scapa Flow in Orkney. We are one of the gateway countries for the sea routes that will soon open through the Arctic, along with Norway, Greenland and Denmark. NATO will want us, if we are willing, to keep an eye on the threat from the North.

In this sector, we punch well below our potential. Apart from oil and gas, the marine sector is less than 2% of the economy, less than 50,000 jobs. The new frontier most relevant for Scotland is not space and the galaxy, but the Arctic and the deep sea. Where are the large companies and research bases to match Norway's? We have no Kongsberg, rich in sub-sea technology, which has hoovered up British marine businesses. We have no merchant shipping fleet anymore. Our fishing fleet is relatively small. Norway has over 6,000 fishing boats, Scotland around 2,000 – similar to Ireland. What is the focus of our Marine Research effort at Universities? Is Aberdeen really looking to the Marine future beyond oil and gas?

As we discussed in Chapter 2, we want to see a concerted new programme to create an ambitious 50-year Marine Industrial and Agricultural Policy, not just in the context of the melting Arctic sea ice. The sea is where the future lies for all sorts of things. 70% of the earth's surface is water, and we are only scratching the surface for marine food for example, with mainly traditional, simple fishing. A new set of players are expected to emerge that are seaweed, asparagus, and fruit and vegetable aquafarmers and marine entrepreneurs in companies such as Agrisea. Strengthening industrial, economic, research, and cultural links with the Nordic nations seems a sensible first step. If you can't beat them, join them!

Novelty is not enough

Invention costs money – innovation makes money

Everyone gets excited about SME's and new start-ups. But to feed a country, novelty is not enough. A complete value creation ecosystem is required: the whole chain from university research to concept demonstration, product and system development, marketing, manufacturing and installation, operations, and product/service support. This needs money: risk tolerant, opportunity seeking money to fund experimentation, recover from dead ends, and accelerate the process right through the value stream; to carry ideas from flaky invention to large-scale, routine, satisfactory, value-creating use; and, at the end of life, to decommission and recycle the old, and replace it with the new – which has gone through the same process.

The path from invention (something that costs money) to innovation (something that makes money) is neither straightforward nor linear. Never a single scientific breakthrough. Many technologies and processes come together, perfectly blended like a well-crafted luxury whisky. Add a twist of luck, test for boring reliability, reach for new ways to use stuff already known. Be prepared for new technology to spawn or enhance many products, in many different market sectors. Silicon chips and liquid crystal displays have wormed their way into almost any product you can imagine, from phones to cameras to home entertainment to cars to washing machines to planes and ships and spacecraft.

Edison, we are told, said "innovation is 1% inspiration and 99% perspiration." Each innovator creates work for many implementers. And it's a two-way street: the implementers need something to implement. The inventor can't turn the clever idea into wealth-creating innovation alone. It takes the input of many people, with many different skills and perspectives.

So, to be clear: to generate sustainable wealth from research outputs we need not just a few clever people, but a whole value-adding ecosystem reliant on the education and skills of a large part of the population. And society, which funds the early research and provides the infrastructure for the innovation ecosystem, deserves its share of the rewards. Too often, as Mazzucato never tires of pointing out, the profits are privatised while the risks are socialised.

Location matters too. The valley south of Annemasse, a French town near Geneva, has one of the highest concentrations of high-tech engineering companies in Europe. The reason is 'location, location, location.' It's on the motorway between Paris and Milan, so it can service both the French and Italian automotive and aerospace industries; and it's at the edge of the Alps, so it's a nice place to live.

Scotland is a nice place to live too, but we lack Annemasse's favourable location. No point trying to compete against well-established businesses in more favourable locations –we succeed by being different, and by capitalising on our unique advantages.

Taking back control?

An important part of rebuilding our engineering business ecosystem is to create Tier One companies, or Prime Contractors, both to run big projects in Scotland, and to export Scottish content overseas. These are the companies that take on big, complex, high-risk projects, choose and manage all the suppliers, get everything working together, and hand the completed job over to the client on time and on budget (ideally), or operate it long-term to provide an agreed service. The contract may even include decommissioning at the end of the asset's life.

There's a lot there to go wrong. It's not easy to deliver a complex project with a good outcome for all the stakeholders: client, end users, the prime contractor and its many subcontractors, the local community, wider society, and the environment. To try to control their risk, public sector clients issue complicated and voluminous requests for quotations (RFQs). Only big companies have the people and knowledge to even read and understand these RFQs, never mind put together a winning response. Many such contracts go badly. Look at the Holyrood parliament building, the Edinburgh tram project, the Queen Elizabeth University Hospital in Glasgow, the new Sick Kids' in Edinburgh, the many problems with school PFIs, and Britain's dismal record in procuring big public sector software projects. The more things go wrong, the more extra clauses get written into the contracts, the fewer companies are able to put together credible responses, and so we spin on round in ever-decreasing circles. The same small group of companies keeps winning a disproportionate share of large public sector contracts, even though those same companies were responsible for the previous poor outcomes. (Hard to credit, isn't it?)

To get more competition, procurers have brought in foreign contractors. The Edinburgh Tram project was performed by a German company. The Queensferry Crossing was built by a consortium of four companies, one Scottish and the others from the US, Spain, and Germany. Scotrail is run by foreign state-owned railway operators. The massive new windfarm at the mouth of the Forth Estuary was launched with great fanfare, then sold to EDF, and will be manufactured almost entirely overseas. It's this last point that particularly hurts: the loss of local jobs and added value at the whim of foreign investors whose only care is maximising profits. We see the same in the private sector. Most of the Scottish fish farming industry is now owned by a Norwegian company. Scotland's excellent defence contractors, the shipbuilders and high-tech electronics manufacturers, are all foreign owned.

We need world-class tier 1 companies operating from and based in Scotland if we are to capture full value from our R, and particularly from our D. This would be a big transformation which would need government intervention not just to facilitate and play honest broker, but to provide what Mariana Mazzucato calls "mission leadership." We suggest in this book six strategic themes the government should be spearheading to transform our economy. We need public procurement working for Scottish businesses. Companies who promise to create jobs in Scotland should be held to those promises. Those that fail to deliver on jobs or on results should not be rewarded with more contracts.

In summary, increased R&D is absolutely critical. But the creation of at least one Scottish Tier One company per strategic sector will be equally important for the future. Germany is an interesting model. Its Mittelstand is made up of very many world-class middle-sized family-owned companies. There would be far fewer, with less investment or less success, without Germany's world-scale manufacturing and prime contracting companies – BMW, Siemens, VW, Bosch, just to mention some of the best-known household names – in their home market.

Descope defence, and…

But how can all this be funded, you ask? Roughly speaking we're talking about Scotland spending an extra two percent of GDP each year on R&D.

The big issue of funding these investments in Scotland's future is largely for another book. However, as a preview of that debate we will suggest three potential ways to raise money for expanding research and development. All three are controversial. Whichever way, we need to find a further 2% of GDP - three billion pounds per annum – to fund this expansion in R&D.

Here we are about to risk the "without the politics" label of this book. Hold your fire for a while. It's important to raise the options and understand them fully. The first is only possible, we think, in a future independent Scotland or a radically restructured federal UK: a total re-examination of defence posture and expenditure. The second (next section) is a strong dose of Keynesian economics. This is back in fashion as a result of Covid-19. After forty years of generally unsuccessful attempts to balance budgets, most nations in the world seem to have decided that government stimulus spending is acceptable again, even if it increases budget deficits. The third is looking to Norway for investment.

Let's look at the defence issue first. Defence, with the exception of military research and development that is useful for the rest of the economy and for defence exports, is largely just a cost – expenditure is written off as it occurs. Secondly, defence is a low-growth sector for most economies, except China and India's perhaps. Certainly, it is not a growing sector for the UK. In contrast, the R&D in growth sectors of the economy that we have identified is an investment which will pay back many times over in wealth, health, and wellbeing. Equally, the other mission-oriented themes we propose for investment in this book are just that – investments, not 'spending.'

The UK still wants to be a 'global power' with 'global reach.' That's reflected in its defence budget and force structure. The defence needs of an independent 21st-century Scotland would be very different. If it were to come into being, one of its first tasks would be to re-orientate its defence organisation to a more appropriate role for a small maritime nation.

In the 2014 referendum, thinking on defence policy for an independent Scotland could be summarised as "let's have eight percent of Britain's armed forces." A moment's thought makes it clear we shouldn't take that too literally. What earthly use would one sixth of an aircraft carrier be to Scotland – or indeed the remaining five-sixths to the rest of the UK?

The 2014 Scottish Government white paper, and the 2018 Sustainable Growth Commission report, suggested that Scotland might have a defence budget of £2.5 Bn, approximately 1.6% of GDP. This is above the European average, but below the 2% target for NATO members.

An independent Scotland would need to be very clear-headed about its position within a European defence context. Why would we not cut Scotland's spending on defence to 1.0% of GDP, more like Sweden's? Or even to 0.5%, like Ireland's? (Yes, we know, NATO. But better to spend 1% on effective capability than 2% on me-too forces that would be too subscale to be effective.)

We believe that three principles should apply to an independent Scotland's defence policy. First, only concern ourselves with real and credible threats to Scotland's integrity and well-being. Second, when we invest in a defence capability, we do it effectively. Achieve a critical mass that gives our services a world-class capability; ensure we can afford to keep our capabilities up to date; and spend the vast majority of the money involved within Scotland. Third, invest in capabilities that complement and enhance, rather than replicate and dilute, those of our close allies.

In our humble view, the wackiest suggestion in prevailing assumptions is that an independent Scotland should maintain a mechanised army brigade, capable of supporting a battalion-sized battle group overseas on UN-type peace-keeping missions. Mechanised battlegroups are good for invading dry flat countries, not for defending boggy hilly ones. For an independent Scotland, being able to deploy a mechanised battlegroup on sustained overseas operations, as has been suggested, with appropriate air transport links home, would distort the whole force structure. Not only would it be very costly, it would be ill adapted to dealing with realistic threats closer to home.

The focus should be, instead, totally on protecting Scotland, its waters and its airspace against credible threats, including hybrid warfare, terrorism, and organised crime. Missions in the rest of the world are incredibly expensive, and of extremely dubious effectiveness. Scotland wouldn't need regular infantry, armoured troop carriers, or long-range transport aircraft. It would need fast-response special forces, capable of mountain, arctic, and marine warfare, liberally equipped with helicopters, boats and UAVs.

That's not all.

The information age offers a host of opportunities to hostile states (and non-state actors) to undermine, subvert, influence, and even control other nations without the need to actually invade the country. Attacks on our financial system and democratic structures and governance are more likely than on our physical assets – and more difficult to detect, understand, and defeat. A key part of a re-oriented defence policy would be cyber and information warfare defences, probably collaborating closely with Estonia and other small tech-savvy European allies as well as the UK; and intelligence, collaborating with the UK.

As we say elsewhere, it's clear from Covid-19 that biosecurity is going to be a key issue from now on. Given that that 'one sick bat' seems to have crashed the world economy and killed hundreds of thousands of people, all countries need to be much better prepared to respond to pandemics – whether due to natural causes or biological warfare – than most were in 2020. Is it also a defence issue that antibiotic resistant bacteria are multiplying, to the extent that current antibiotics are becoming useless faster than we are inventing new ones?

A Scottish navy would need ships able to operate throughout its waters, extending 200 miles offshore in one of the most hostile oceans in the world. It would not by itself be able to fight off a serious attack by a big navy – but that's what alliances are for. The key in modern warfare is information. Scotland has world-class sensing, networking, and information processing capabilities, thanks to three key synergistic elements: long-established high-tech defence companies (Leonardo and Thales); an excellent world-level research and teaching base; and the recently established innovation centres seeking avenues to exploit advanced university research on sensors (CENSIS) and data science (The Data Lab). And our oil and gas industry has huge expertise in subsea operations.

We think a major part of Scotland's future defence budget should be used to fund an ambitious and futuristic underwater sensing programme, leveraging these assets to create an integrated underwater surveillance system that lets us spot any military or environmental threat anywhere in or near our waters. This will be more important as the Arctic sea routes open up, and would boost our high-tech industry and exports. Export prospects might include Sweden, which is frequently embarrassed by incursions (actual or imagined) by Russian submarines in its coastal waters. By having the development capability in-country we would ensure the system would be adapted to Scotland's needs, and continue to evolve as technology improves.

Whatever the politics, we need an air interception capability to patrol airspace and see off intruding Russians. Air defence of the British Isles is one area of defence in which an independent Scotland's interests seem to be absolutely aligned with those of the rest of the UK. We would encourage the RAF to continue to use Lossiemouth for its Typhoon squadrons, and to operate the long-range radars and electronic surveillance kit on various Scottish sites. We could be delegating our air defence back to the UK in return for our efforts to radically enhance underwater surveillance capabilities.

Instead of being a net drain on Scotland's economy, defence expenditure could be less than at present, boost indigenous high-tech industry, and provide a valuable new capability to our allies. Spending more on R&D and less on expensive military platforms, and eschewing foreign military adventures, would keep more of the defence budget within the Scottish economy, increase the multiplier effect that our defence spending has on the rest of the economy, and contribute more to the defence of the British Isles and Europe.

Little of this rebalancing is an option as long as responsibility for defence and foreign affairs remains reserved to Westminster. If that were the case, we would simply seek that Defence Industrial policy is more aligned to Scotland's other industrial R&D interests and those of the six sectors that are part of the vision.

Return to Keynesian economics?

We aren't economists. We view economics in simplistic terms. We would definitely fail a final economic undergraduate exam and it's far too late for us to become chief economists, but here goes.

The austerity imposed on the UK after the 2007-8 financial crisis was pure neoliberalism. To us, that means unfettered free markets, low taxes, and a government that keeps its budget balanced and only intervenes in markets to keep commerce flowing.

The massive economic stimulus that governments are launching to sustain and restart their economies after the Covid-19 pandemic is pure Keynesianism, named after the famous British economist John Maynard Keynes, who rose to prominence in the 1930s. It takes the view that not only should the state be proactive in preventing market failures, and in regulating the "free" market; but also, in stimulating the economy when there isn't enough private sector activity to keep people employed. Government spending has a beneficial multiplier effect because of the way money spent initially by government then moves through the economy. Keynesianism was the default economic position after World War 2 until the 70s, when economic problems started to multiply.

Let's clarify one point. There is enough work to do to improve society and the environment that there's no need for meaningless make-work to form any part of stimulus spending. If there's nothing else needing done, employ more teachers to reduce pupil-teacher ratios, more carers the better to look after the old and disabled, and pay everyone else to go back to school or college to acquire new skills.

Modern Monetary Theory[12] (MMT) is a different way of thinking about money rather than a different economic policy. To its advocates, budget deficits are not a problem. They say the whole language of deficits and the claimed equivalence between national and household budgets are the wrong framing.

We have been looking carefully at MMT, and there are a couple of points we want to understand better before forming a strong view. In particular, it seems to underplay the issues around foreign currency reserves and exchange rates that have dominated economic discussions for much of our, the authors', lives.

The simple MMT arguments seem to work in a country that:

- is more or less self-sufficient in the essentials of its society;
- hasn't accumulated a mass of foreign currency debt;

- can afford to stop spending foreign currency on imports if its own currency loses value.

To be in this happy state, as far as we can make out, you need to export as much stuff that's essential to others as you need to import stuff that's essential to you; and you need to agree all public sector contracts in your own currency, not someone else's.

If you can achieve this, you won't be critically dependent on a favourable and stable exchange rate – and your currency will probably tend to be strong anyway, so it's not going to be a problem. Britain's currency has been in remorseless decline against the US Dollar since WW2 because we took on a huge amount of dollar debt during and after WW2, which we have only recently paid off.

An independent Scotland would probably be able to balance exports and imports quite happily, though it might need to bring some high value manufacture back onshore to achieve that. It would need to avoid burdening itself with lots of Sterling or Euro or Dollar debt.

A federal Scotland would need to have borrowing powers and appropriate governance to be able to commit to major spending or investment out of step with the rest of the UK. Currently, the magic of Barnett Formula consequentials means that when the UK does stimulus spending, Scotland can too, in equal proportion. But when the UK turns off the tap, it turns it off for Scotland too. If our economy is out of phase with the rest of the UK's, then the timing of the UK's stimulus spending would be out of phase with our needs. Hence the esoteric arguments about borrowing powers for devolved governments and local authorities.

Would Norway's Sovereign Fund invest in Scotland?

As part of looking North, Norway is an obvious partner for many parts of this vision – the melting Arctic sea ice, the common challenge of greater forestation, the interest in marine technologies, the need to diversify away from oil, and small populations seeking to invest in the future tech world. The big difference is Norway has a huge surplus of funds, and Scotland (and the UK) is seriously short of surplus funds. In simplistic terms there is clearly a match here. Norway can benefit from long-term diversified investment, while Scotland needs substantial short-term funding, especially post-Covid-19.

Again, we are straying into geo-politics. However, we think, if you let your imagination run away under any constitutional scenario, you can see the merit of approaching Norway at an inter-Governmental level to promote this vision and potentially convince them to support the funding of extra R&D, forestation, marine research, and cooperation in the new north-east trading route.

A deep dive into technology, 2055

Remember Frank and his colleagues on the train in our story in Chapter 1? Imagine they invested strongly in Scottish tech opportunities and stayed the course to turn these companies into world beaters. Imagine if the Hypertel® technology that appeared at the end of Chapter 2 had been one of these home-grown successes. How might part of that story play?

***

The expert witness at the Board of Inquiry about the near-miss incident (in the story at the end of Chapter 2) was Rognvald Heddle's young cousin. She was all dressed up posh and looking respectable, and he didn't recognise her at first. The last time they'd met she was about 15, visiting Orkney on a family holiday, wet hair all over the place, wearing a wetsuit, and chasing after him on a jet ski. Rognvald was thrilled because her evidence had cleared his colleague, and also looked like it would be improving the way they worked. They had a long chat after the Board of Inquiry hearing was over.

"The thing is, Rognvald, artificial intelligence is just that – artificial. It doesn't work the same way we do, and needs different information, presented in a different order, to make a given decision. So, when the AI system gave up, there was no point giving the human pilot the same information the AI system hadn't been able to make any sense of – because the human couldn't make any sense of it either. The human needed different kinds of cues to get orientated and make sense of the situation. Give him a video picture and an AIS display on a map, and he'd make sense of it in a few seconds. Give him the more abstract data the AI system uses, and it took him the best part of a minute to get himself orientated. He couldn't start dealing with the situation until he understood it – and that takes time. In planes, they reckon it takes about 20 seconds for a human to take over from an automatic system, or even another pilot, so it's absolutely essential that he doesn't have to make any critical decisions within that time."

"Hmm. You've learnt a bit since we last met."

"When did we last see each other?"

"That time you were up here on holiday, and we borrowed those jet skis, and went racing all over Scapa Flow until you ran out of fuel!"

"Oh my god! That was so embarrassing. Your Dad was furious, 'cause the pilot boat ended up rescuing us, and he got such a ribbing. But it was such brilliant fun."

"Aye, it's lucky they didn't hold it against me when I applied here for a job a few years later. But you're ducking the question – how do you know all that stuff?"

"Well, after I left school, I did a control systems engineering degree in Glasgow. Then I got accepted on the first tranche of the Cognitive Systems Engineering Doctoral Programme at Edinburgh. It was a fantastic programme, all about how people think in concepts before they even start formulating their thoughts into language. There was a lot about how humans absorb information and put it in context – what we call "orientation" – that's why I got to be the expert witness today. But the real stuff is much deeper. I'm working for a company called Hypertel now. They sponsored my doctoral degree and offered me a job as soon as I finished writing up. I've been there for ten years, and now I'm head of their Cognitive Systems Engineering Department."

"Gosh, that sounds awfully grand! What do you do?"

"Run a team of engineers to sort out the machine-brain interactions of this new product we're developing. I do a lot of the work myself. I've got several patents in my name, and I've got a really brilliant team working for me. We're developing a system that will let you communicate with someone else by picking up your brain waves and transferring the thought patterns to the other person, without having to turn it into language."

"So does that mean I can communicate with someone who doesn't speak my language?"

"Exactly. Or with someone who's had a stroke, and whose language centre isn't working properly."

"But – if the other person can see into my brain, how do I stop them reading my private thoughts, things I don't want them to know?"

"Exactly the right question, cousin. Do you want a job?" They both laughed.

"That's what my patents are about. The company founder invented this thing we call the "Ethics Module," and that's what my team is working on perfecting. The principle is a bit like those funny animals that the human characters have with them in the Philip Pullman books – Daemons, he calls them. We create a sort of artificial Daemon, for each person in the conversation. Your Daemon is responsible for making sure none of your inner thinking is exposed to anyone else in a way that's against your interests. So the Daemons have a sort of conversation with their person first, to find out what they are willing to discuss, how they feel, and their motivations; and then the Daemons communicate with each other to sort of feel each other out, and set the ground rules for the interaction.

"My patents are about a self-checking routine that means that if any member of the conversation starts breaking the rules, or gets unhappy with the way things are going, or is distracted thinking about something private, then the link just sort of fades, and only comes back up again when everyone is back in the right frame of mind, as it were. It's absolutely impossible for anyone to use the system in a way that's against the interests of any of the other participants. It's really important you can't use it as an interrogation system for example, or to con little old gentlemen out of their life savings."

"Not little old ladies?" asked Rognvald.

"Nah, we're too smart!"

"Aye well, you've got something there, you with your doctorate and your patents, and me with my master's ticket and blistered hands! And I thought you were just my wee cousin. Where are you staying now? Did you have to move away for this job?"

"No, it's just down the road from Mum and Dad's house, in Dumfries."

160

She changed the subject. "So, tell me more about your job! How did you use to do it in the old days? How did it change with this new automated system you've been using? How would it be done if you could wave a magic wand and get exactly what you wanted?"

Six months later, Rognvald's boss called him in and told him he was going to have to see more of his family. After savouring the shock on his face for a moment, his boss explained that Hypertel had been awarded a contract to develop a new piloting system to replace the one they'd stopped using after the near miss. His cousin had asked for him to be made available as a subject matter expert to help with the development and make sure it would work properly this time. The conversation with her had given her most of the information she needed to specify the system. Could he please help to perfect it?

So he did, and he had lots of video conferences and several trips to Dumfries, staying with his Aunt and Uncle, whom he also hadn't seen for over 20 years.

That was another big change in modern Scotland. The journey from Orkney to Dumfries took a whole day in his Dad's time. By 2055, with the new ultra-high-speed Hyperloop network, it only took a couple of hours to get from one end of the country to the other.

References for Chapter 6

[1] My Scotland, Our Britain, Gordon Brown, Simon & Schuster, 2014

[2] Scottish Sustainable growth Commission Report: Scotland – The New Case for Optimism - *A strategy for inter-generational economic renaissance.* The Sustainable growth Commission, May 2018 https://www.sustainablegrowthcommission.scot/report

[3] Stephen Maxwell, Arguing for Independence – Evidence, Risk, and the Wicked Issues, Luath Press, 2012 &2013

[4] The UK's Finance Curse? Costs and Processes http://speri.dept.shef.ac.uk/2018/10/05/uk-finance-curse-report/ Sheffield Political Economy Research Institute, 2019

[5] Scotland in 2050 - Realising our Global Potential. Fraser of Allander Institute, March 2019

[6] *Scotland's Financial Services Expertise*, Scottish Financial Enterprise, October 2018

[7] For a fully thought out and costed example, see Common Weal, *The Common Home Plan*, November 2019

[8] Mariana Mazzucato, The Entrepreneurial State, Penguin, 2013

[9] *Scotland's Financial Services Expertise*, Scottish Financial Enterprise, October 2018

[10] As of March 20th, 2020. https://en.wikipedia.org/wiki/Global_Financial_Centres_Index

[11] https://www.insider.co.uk/news/treasury-select-committee-chair-nicky-12057558

[12] For the arguments for MMT, see for example Stephanie Keaton's very readable book *The Deficit Myth: Modern monetary Theory and how to build a better economy*, John Murray, June 2020. For some of the criticisms, see for example Fullbrook and Morgan, *Modern Monetary Theory and its critics, WEA,* Feb 2020. Both also available on Kindle.

Chapter 7

Infrastructure – virtual is the new reality!

Wood is the new steel!

Our vision for a new generation of Scotland's infrastructure: world-scale universities and airports; electric planes and helicopters; wood based, super-insulated buildings; the fastest broadband in the world; and a modern high-speed public transport network connecting car-free city and town centres throughout the land. We're all connected in Scotland's Virtual City – fuelled by wind and tide, built of wood and stone, linked by rail and optical fibre, and united by shared culture and values.

Back to the future!

The next time Simon and John spoke on Zoom, Simon remembered to unmute the microphone. This time, it was John, who had borrowed his brother's holiday home near Nethy Bridge for a couple of months, who was disadvantaged by the technology.

"Hi John, what's it like being back in the Highlands?"

"It's beautiful! I'd forgotten just how lovely it is at this time of year. But it's like going back to last century. I'm going to write to the Chairman of my brother's network provider and threaten to take them to court for misrepresentation. Call it 'broadband'! Only in the most fevered imagination of the most mendacious advertising executive in the world could the bandwidth here be described as 'broad'! Impossible to do business from here, just impossible."

Simon smiled at the exaggeration. "What bandwidth have you got?"

"Nought point four megabits at the moment. The best we ever get is just over two. They claim five, but that's ridiculous!" replied John. Simon did a double take. John wasn't exaggerating after all.

"Hmm. We get 100 megs, and we could get 300 if we paid through the nose. Your video looks really fuzzy, and the sound's pretty bad. This was easier when you were in Abu Dhabi!"

"Why do you think we abandoned the idea of setting up our engineering consultancy business here in the Spey valley? Simply impossible because of the lousy internet connection – not to mention three hours to Edinburgh airport. Longer to Glasgow. Inverness airport: not even a connection to Heathrow at one point! Saving the Caledonian sleeper not quite enough to revitalise the area's economy."

John continued his rant. "Three hours from Aviemore to my oil clients in Aberdeen. Seven hours from Glasgow to Thurso and Wick, sometimes more. It's easier to get to Dubai!"

Simon sounded a voice of reason. "Well, at least you can fly there direct from Scotland now. I remember 50 years ago, the only overseas destination you could fly to direct from Edinburgh was Ireland!"

Still John would not be mollified. "But have you ever tried coming off an international flight at Glasgow and travelling through to Stirling or Edinburgh? With jetlag? It's a total nightmare!"

Simon returned to the safer ground of communications. "At least the R100 programme aims to roll out 'superfast' broadband to 100% of the Scottish population. Mind you, so-called superfast is only 30 megabits per second. I've got 100, and even that's not particularly fast in today's world.

"But think back fifty years! I remember being on holiday in Skye in the early 70s, and I ran out of money. I phoned my Dad – remember those awful 'Press button A – now press button B' public phones? – and asked him to telegraph money for me to Glenbrittle post office. Next day I picked up four well-used one-pound notes to keep me going til the end of the holiday. Who could have imagined mobile phones, or the internet, then?"

John turned philosophical. "It's funny how some things have changed kind of predictably; some things we absolutely take for granted were pure science fiction 50 years ago; and some things really haven't changed at all."

"Yes, trying to predict 50 years ahead is a mug's game. But you have to do it, because infrastructure has a design life of 100 years! Maybe you have to think like a science fiction writer, not a project manager. My engineer friends tell me that if you can imagine it, they can usually find a way to do it. Except for nuclear fusion, of course. When I was at University in the 70s, that was going to give the whole human race an abundant supply of free energy within thirty years. And it's still 30 years away now, in 2020!"

John added, "I have been involved a little in the new City, NEOM. Located in the empty desert on the Red Sea in Saudi. A population the size of Glasgow in ten years. Amazing ambition. 'First Cognitive City built on 5G Technology.' '40% of the world's population can reach it in 4 hours.' The strapline I like the best. 'Combining Silicon Valley, Dubai and the Seychelles.'"

"Sounds like a Highland Broadband promise to me!"

John continued. "Maybe, but a real attempt by some architects to change the way they think. Design, overdesign in fact, the digital component of a city, then seek the minimum physical infrastructure to support it. I suppose this is much easier if you start from scratch with an empty desert. Not so easy for a legacy city."

"Scotland has plenty of empty wet desert!" Simon pointed out.

"You're right," John replied. But Scotland hasn't got the $500 billion allocated for Saudi's future 2030 Vision. We'd have to find more money from somewhere."

"A bit of a dilemma. How much on NHS? How much on the renewables? How much on physical infrastructure? How about we abandon HS2 and Trident?" added Simon.

John continued, "Now we are getting down to the nub of it. There are those who want to leave the country untouched. The beauty of the wilderness. No pylons, no upgrades to the A9, no ugly windmills in the beauty spots. Walking in the hills, sailing the beautiful islands, and taking slow trains to nowhere. Yet others, like me, who worry about connectivity, international travel, broadband speed in the Highlands, being at the heart of the world's next big technological steps. Quite a dilemma for the planners and politicians, I guess. No winners there."

How much should we spend on infrastructure?

The UK Government classes infrastructure as transport, energy, utilities, digital infrastructure, science & research, flood and coastal erosion defences, and social infrastructure. The total infrastructure spend reported by the UK Government[1] runs at around £60 bn a year, or £5bn a month, split about 50/50 between private and public sectors. Scotland, as part of the UK, has fallen way behind in infrastructure versus the Netherlands, France, Japan, Korea, Singapore, and now China, and this decline is likely to continue.

While billions are being spent on HS2 and Crossrail in Southern England, the mainly single-track rail line to Inverness still requires 3 hours for just 130 miles. The current improvement programme will allow increased frequency but not increased speeds. Published figures for infrastructure investment are very difficult to unravel because of different assumptions and different planning horizons. A recent IPPR North report estimates that London gets three times as much transport investment per capita as the North, six times as much as Yorkshire and Humberside. This required forensic analysis of the data to understand, not least because the enormous spending by Transport for London is excluded on the grounds that it's funded from revenue. We provide references in the footnotes for anyone wishing to delve deeper[2].

Scotland has had quite a high per capita spend on transport and energy infrastructure for the last few years because of the Queensferry Crossing, the Edinburgh to Glasgow rail Improvement Programme (EGIP), and the massive offshore windfarms. Unfortunately, the local work content is relatively low. This must change.

However, before we simply make a plea for more infrastructure spending over a 50-year period, let's step back and think laterally about what we are asking for. Lord Nicholas Stern – Professor of Economics and Government at the LSE, and Chair of the Grantham Research Institute on Climate Change and the Environment – states that the key challenge in a future economy is to decouple economic growth from environmental destruction. He suggests three critical actions[3]: to raise energy productivity growth in the economy from the current 1.7% per annum to 3% per annum; to introduce a carbon tax at a level of $40-80 per tonne and raise that further to $50-100 by 2030; and finally, to introduce radical redesign into the expansion of cities and infrastructure. Sustainable infrastructure is the new mantra.

Future infrastructure, if it is to meet our future needs, will require radicalism, starting now. For example, it's sensible to aim as soon as possible for a network of all-electric aircraft to serve the short-haul flights within Scotland. And let's design a much more efficient rail system that is not simply reliant on incremental improvements to historic tracks. (Assuming that mass transit systems remain viable – at the current stage of the Covid-19 epidemic, it's not at all clear when most people will be willing to travel in crowded trains and planes again. Thinking more futuristically, it also begs the question of whether we should hold off to see if Elon Musk's Hyperloop concept turns into reality.)

Current building practices in the UK are so 20th-century. It's time to stop building suburban estates of expensive-to-heat detached houses with 3-4 bedrooms and two or three concrete car parking spaces. These do not delink economic growth from carbon emissions.

Instead, encourage low-level, affordable, high-quality apartment complexes built with Scottish wood. Insist on Passiv Haus insulation levels for all new buildings to reduce energy bills by 90%. Why not provide more vertical gardens and rooftop gardens instead of patches surrounding detached houses? We can reduce heating costs and improve energy efficiency further with collective heating and hot water systems, the water pre-heated in solar thermal panels integrated into the building structures. Ban personal cars from city centres, and put housing and social facilities near our workplaces, so that most folk can walk or cycle to work. Work hubs in each town and village would allow those able to work remotely to get out of the house, have the social benefit of meeting other people at work, and access decent broadband and printing facilities.

All of this underpinned and enabled by continued and accelerating investment in digital connectivity – optical fibre, 5G, and 6G if and when it comes. As far as digitising our administration is concerned, the UK's track record in that area isn't brilliant, with overspends and outright failures in too many key government IT programmes; though there are honourable exceptions such as DVLA. Interestingly, Estonia seems to be the country to learn from – a small country of 1.3 million people, but an 'internet Titan[4]' and recognised leader in the internet economy. Estonia committed very early after independence in 1991 to digitising the country and as much of its administration as possible – among other reasons, because it doesn't have enough people to run a traditional paper-based government bureaucracy. As a result, at the start of the Covid-19 pandemic, the education system switched quickly and relatively painlessly to digital education[5].

From Skyscrapers to Plyscrapers: wood is the new steel

We now have the opportunity to introduce much more radical design into the building of new housing and new cities. New technologies are available for making fireproof structural elements as strong as steel out of – believe it or not – wood.

We are at the start of a material revolution. Forward to the past. Concrete and steel construction, responsible for about 8% of the world's carbon footprint, has seen its peak.

The prominent and controversial concrete structures of the 1960s that appeared in many parts of Scotland, notably replacing Edinburgh's Georgian architectural heritage in parts of Princes Street and George Square, should be a thing of the past. Energy intensive bricks are antiques. Whatever you think of Prince Charles' 'monstrous carbuncles', love them or hate them, it's time to move on.

In case you think we are condemning Scotland to the adoption of hand-built, Amish style Pennsylvanian barns, or thin-walled, fire risky, mid-American bungalows blown over in a gale, or poorly constructed villages modelled off cheap African houses, then think again. We are talking about a building called T3 in Minneapolis built in 2017, a 7-storey modern commercial block with over 220,000 square feet of floor space; or an 18-story high-rise apartment complex in Vancouver, also built in 2017, called Brock Commons. Anders Berensson Architects designed 31 cross-laminated timber (CLT) buildings, stronger than steel, built on Stockholm's waterfront. A 436-foot high-rise wooden building is to follow, also in Stockholm. And glue-laminated wood (Glulam) or Laminated Veneer Lumber (LVL) high-rise buildings are as fire retardant as steel buildings. Plus, the structural material itself is insulating, so there's no need for the lethal Grenfell-style add-on insulation cladding.

Combining this material revolution with the other key 21st-century building technology, offsite manufacture of major assemblies, Norway built an 18-storey wooden tower block at the astonishing pace of nearly a floor a week[6]. We can do the same here in Scotland.

We are talking about a new generation of Scottish based architects and designers with an image of the Swedes for wood-based thinking, using a boom in the local Scottish marketplace to get started, with aspirations to expand to serve non-wood dominated countries such as England and France.

But this architectural "oil tanker" will take a long time to turn – unless, of course, Governments kick off the revolution, big time. A case for Scottish regulations to be futuristic and draconian. What about a total ban on non-wood buildings in the next decade? That would set us off on a very different path immediately.

And we can be sure of one thing: the world's Timber Age will not come to an end, because we won't run out of timber – especially in Scotland, where we will be planting 5 billion over the next few decades and where at least 3% of the economy will be based on wood products. This is a no-brainer for Scotland, but Scotland has a habit of not doing the obvious.

Imagine the central belt as one virtual city

Scotland as one city region

Scotland also faces another issue as it contemplates future infrastructure spending. Its two biggest cities, Glasgow and Edinburgh, are very close together, unlike many other countries, such as England, or Germany, or Italy, or the USA. Why not think more radically of the whole central belt as a single, virtual city of over 2 million people? Eliminate duplicate infrastructure, such as airports, Universities, leadership institutions, Government offices, and communications. Eliminate the East/West rivalry that has shaped a lot of Scotland's investment thinking. Combine them as a single virtual city to become competitive with larger nearby cities such as Manchester and Birmingham. Think and act as a single international hub, comparable with Stockholm's role in Sweden, or Helsinki's in Finland, or Oslo's in Norway.

This has to go beyond the M8 corridor. Imagine Scotland re-establishing its engineering prowess by setting up major medical and marine technology and engineering centres in Glasgow, Inverness, Dundee, Dumfries, and Aberdeen: becoming an engineering powerhouse for the 21st century, using our energy and ingenuity to create the Scotland we want to bequeath to our grandchildren.

To plan the journey, we can't look forward from where we are right now, and still less can we keep looking to the past: instead, let's leap forward fifty years in our imagination, imagine things as we would want them to be, and then look back from there to see how we got there.

But vision is not enough. Better specification, better governance, and better oversight of contracts are equally important. The embarrassingly expensive and inflexible PFIs of recent times are outdated, especially since we can take full advantage of the public sector's ability to borrow at such low interest rates, lower than the private sector. A rethink of the planning and valuation process is overdue. For example, the public sector should share the benefit of the uplift in land values that happens when land is re-zoned – by the public sector – for infrastructure development.

Bigger cities are wealthier

Scotland has a total population of 5 million people, a number which is not expected to grow much in the next 50 years, spread across 32 unitary authority areas. Its major cities are not large by world standards, and they compete against each other for resources and status. The feeling of separateness is exacerbated by the high cost of transport: rail travel between the two largest towns, Edinburgh and Glasgow, only 50 miles apart, is among the most expensive per mile anywhere[7].

68 cities in the world have greater than five million people. 10 cities already have populations of over twenty million people, and we expect urbanisation to continue. By 2070, when world population is expected to peak, there might be 40 megacities with a population of over 20 million. Successful bigger cities have stronger economies, and experience faster economic growth. Reasons include the economies of scale in manufacturing and infrastructure, cross fertilisation of technologies and innovation, and more vibrant social life. Because of their prosperity, people flock to them – making them even bigger. Recent studies estimate[8] that every doubling of a city's population, other things being equal, increases productivity per head by 15%.

Edinburgh and Glasgow are already quite successful in UK terms. They are respectively third and fifth in the league table of UK cities ranked by GVA per head of population[9]. London is first, Milton Keynes second, and Belfast fourth. But if you could magically merge Edinburgh and Glasgow, it seems you could increase the GVA of the combined population by 15%, that's to say from the current £34k/head averaged across the two cities to nearer £39k/head. (Currently Edinburgh is £37k and Glasgow £32k). If we could even more magically add the other 3.5 million Scots to the combined population of Edinburgh and Glasgow, there would be a potential increase in wealth of another 30%. Of course, all of these figures need to be taken with a considerable pinch of salt, because generally other things aren't equal –but it's an interesting line of reasoning.

We wouldn't for a moment suggest another round of clearances, to migrate all of Scotland's population to the central belt and fill the countryside between Edinburgh and Glasgow with concrete. Nor would we propose migrating all of Scotland's research and technology activity to a single, world-scale tech centre in the middle of the central belt. This would be inadvisable for many reasons – migration costs for physical assets, loss of history and tradition, brand loss, and further brain drains to mention but a few.

But there is another way. Think virtual! Scotland could start to think and act as a virtual City State of 5 million people, a super-charged Singapore (population similar, at 5.7m), but unlike Singapore, with a resource-rich hinterland. Superb, integrated, and affordable internet and public transport throughout the country could dissolve distance and social barriers between the different population centres. If there is one thing we've learnt in the Covid-19 epidemic, it's that virtual working is much more feasible for many people and jobs than had been realised. Virtual scale-up may be the new reality.

The whole of Scotland is the size of a small-to-medium-size city. Its University and Tech centres feel even smaller. Its airports are regional rather than international hubs. Its university medical hospitals have slipped from being in the top three in the world at the time of World War 1 to somewhere around number 20. Can virtualisation help?

It's not just cities, it's city regions

City region is a relatively new term coined by planners to describe a city with its hinterland. A city alone can't sustain itself without importing food, water, and energy. Potentially, a city region, a city with a rural hinterland and satellite towns, can be fully self-sustaining – wealth from the city, resources from the hinterland.

San Jose, the epicentre of Silicon Valley, has a population of about a million, not much more than Glasgow. The Bay area as a whole has a population approaching 8 million, and is full of financiers, entrepreneurs, engineers, and supportive Government agencies. San Jose University and Berkeley University have similar sizes to Edinburgh and Glasgow, but the real challenge is that Stanford University alone is 30 times better funded than the Universities of Edinburgh and Glasgow combined. The wider hinterland of Northern California provides food, water, energy, outdoor recreation – and wine! – in abundance.

Not only is Scotland smaller in population than the Bay Area, but it doesn't think of itself as one city region. Two competing major cities, several more significant cities and large towns, 32 separate unitary authorities. Scotland's research and technology infrastructure is scattered throughout the country and doesn't have the power of a single, integrated tech centre like San Jose's Silicon Valley, or Boston's high-tech cluster drawing on the powerful campuses of Harvard and MIT.

Small is beautiful, but attractive as it may seem, don't expect economic health and wealth from the current cricket team of universities – and the solution certainly isn't further decentralisation, devolving small-scale tech centres to local communities. That's not the way wealth-generating tech innovation works. Even Sweden and Finland have a much more consolidated structure as a starting point. Sweden has ten major industrial companies of international stature. Scotland has…?

Collaborate and concentrate to excel

Airports

By modern standards, Scotland is losing out by spreading itself too thinly, and not collaborating to create the critical mass that would allow us to excel. Two examples to consider, absolutely key to this ambitious step, but highly controversial due to deeply entrenched vested interests, are airports and universities.

Scotland would benefit greatly from creating a single European-scale airport hub between Edinburgh and Glasgow. This consolidation would improve productivity and put Scotland on the European map – a high-quality hub to compete with Dublin and Copenhagen. It might also, under certain circumstances, reduce the carbon footprint of air travel: first, by eliminating duplicate flights to the same destination from the two airports; and second, by removing the need for transit flights via London for "thicker" routes where there is enough traffic from Scotland as a whole to justify a direct flight, but not enough from the catchment area of either of the two existing main airports.

There was a recommendation in 1939 to build a Central Scotland airport in Inchyra Park to serve both cities. However, the war got in the way of its development. Post war, other priorities for investment in an essentially bankrupt country took precedence. The Inchyra site was repurposed in 1955.

In 2003 the question was re-opened[10]. The high costs of "airport fragmentation" – having multiple sub-scale airports instead of a single recognised hub with optimised ground transport connections – were identified, but the capital cost was deemed too high. Adding a second runway at Edinburgh in the 2023 timeframe would give a better return on investment. This has not been accomplished yet, but the land required has been kept available. The other conclusion was a call for a direct fast train link between Glasgow's airport, which is on the "wrong" side of the city, and Edinburgh Airport. The train link never happened. The 2003 analysis compared a brand-new site near Airth with incremental improvements to the two existing airports. The incremental option won. But continual short-term thinking of this nature often ends up with poorer quality or more expensive solutions in the long term.

With the new perspective offered to us by climate, we now need to consider the possibility that both the current Glasgow airport and the proposed greenfield site at Airth may eventually be under water. The aviation industry expects air travel numbers to take several years to get back to pre-pandemic levels. Business air travel may never recover to previous levels, now that accountants have discovered how much time and money can be saved by making full use of digital communications.

It's now worth giving serious consideration to making Edinburgh Airport the Central Scotland Airport, drastically upgrading ground transport links with Glasgow and its western hinterland, building the second runway if and when needed, and using the Glasgow airport site for other purposes. A Central Scotland Airport could become a focal point for a much more efficient air and ground transport infrastructure for central Scotland. This single new hub could be linked by fast train to St Pancras and Europe and all the main towns and cities throughout Scotland, benefiting business travellers and tourists alike. This new infrastructure would contribute to the ambitious plans to reduce carbon footprint and put Scotland on the European map as an easy and efficient place to visit.

This of course assumes that air travel recovers after the Covid-19 crisis. If it doesn't, it's questionable whether both Glasgow and Edinburgh airports could be profitable, and the economic case for a single Central Scotland Airport would become even more compelling.

Universities

Similarly, Scotland's universities have to compete internationally for new technological investment and funding. The competition for endowment funds is causing a major challenge to traditional Universities' definition of scale. Oxford and Cambridge's funds of over £1.2bn each have set a new UK benchmark – and this is nowhere near the funding the USA's top universities are attracting. Stanford has an endowment fund of $28 billion and growing. Subscale, separate, and competing, Scotland's current university set-up dilutes excellence, increases overheads, and fragments Government funding. A consolidation would challenge the vested interests of academics, alumni. and politicians, and be unwelcome to many; but the alternative is continuing relative decline if the status quo persists.

It's very simple. Just now, Scotland's fourteen universities compete against each other and other UK universities for available funding in what is not much better than a zero-sum game. This won't keep us at the forefront of research, won't attract the best international talent, and won't give the best possible opportunities to our own students and businesses.

There's no reason why Scotland's university sector can't match the scale and ambition of excellent universities elsewhere – but it needs to work together to build and nurture internationally-recognised centres of excellence. That working together isn't happening, at least not consistently, systematically, and at the required scale. Time for a rethink.

The whole of Scotland has the population of a medium-sized international city. Does Singapore, with its 5.7 million people, have 14 universities? No, and Scotland shouldn't either. The current fragmented system looks to the past (600 years of honourable tradition), rather than to the future of increasingly intense international competition from well-funded institutions in the Middle East, USA, and China.

A single virtual University of Scotland could achieve a critical mass to build on, and increase the current level of high-impact international quality research, while providing redesigned curricula for academic, professional, and vocational education across its different campuses throughout the country. We see no viable alternative in the long term.

Technology centres

At the same time, there would be great merit in investing in a Northern powerhouse based on Green technologies. Not Manchester, as Londoners describe the North, but Inverness, 570 miles north of London and 140 miles north of the traditional Scottish industrial belt. In fact, Inverness, combined with Stornoway in Lewis, Kirkwall in Orkney, and Lerwick in Shetland, could become the leading light for the North of Scotland and the Arctic regions. A showcase for Green cities, modelled off Masdar City in the UAE, and perhaps even funded partly by that ambitious and wealthy country. Renewable energy, a centre of geo-engineering and science, linked to the trading ports in Orkney and Shetland resurrected by the new Northern Sea Route. A race with Copenhagen to create the first fully Green City in Europe.

Transport assets

To take a smaller scale example, the Calmac ferry routes in the Western Isles would also benefit from some whole-system, big-picture, and long-term thinking. Currently, the company runs a hotchpotch of different designs of ship, procured one or two at a time, from different yards, each designed to a unique specification matched to the specific route it's intended for. This may make sense on a short-term view, on a boat-by-boat or route-by-route level, but it doesn't make sense if we consider the whole network of Calmac routes as a single system. The problem is plain to see when one of the vessels on a busy route is out of action for unscheduled maintenance – a depressingly common occurrence. Because each vessel is different, it's difficult to organise a suitable replacement, and this usually involves disrupting other services. Maintenance is difficult and expensive because the multiplicity of boat designs increases the number of spare parts needed to cover the fleet. There is little scope for progressively improving cost and reliability through incremental improvements over a production series. The fleet is reminiscent of the British Airways aircraft fleet in the 80s, with many different types and sizes of planes and a plethora of different seating configurations.

Compare the Easyjet and Ryanair models now. Each airline has standardised on one or two plane types, with standard cabin sizes. Thus, any plane can fly any route, the maintainers have only one type of aircraft to maintain, the airline gets a better price from suppliers, spares holdings are simplified, reliability across the fleet is enhanced, and a few aircraft kept on standby can provide back-up for the entire fleet.

Back at sea, the Norwegian Hurtigruten fast ferry company has a similar policy. All its ferries are similar. New batches of ships are bought every few years to an evolving standard design. All ships of each batch are identical, so they get similar benefits to the one-design airline model we have just described. It's a bit more difficult for Calmac to do this because not all of its routes carry similar levels of traffic; but it would seem to the informed observer that it would be possible to restructure the fleet around a couple of standard designs, and refine these over time to get the benefits of scale and consistency that Hurtigruten, Easyjet, and Ryanair have achieved, and are unattainable with the current heterogeneous fleet.

Centralise or localise? – the inevitable tension

In this chapter we emphasise the benefits of concentration to create the critical mass necessary to succeed at a world scale. This concentration, and the related tendency for central control, creates a tension with the valid arguments for more localisation[11]. Lesley Riddoch's book 'Blossom' argues for doing things for communities in communities, by the communities themselves[12]. She is fond of quoting the statistic that Scotland has the largest local government areas, in terms of population managed by the lowest level of local government organisation, in Europe. This probably isn't a good thing. But on the other hand, it suggests there is plenty of room to do better!

All three authors believe that support of the front line and reduced levels of management are a good thing, and two of the authors argued for such approaches in their previous books. In the real and infinitely complex world, the balance between central control and localisation has been a tension from the beginning of human civilisation. The Roman empire was built on a mix of both concepts, as was the British Empire. The search for the twin benefits from world scale and local empowerment, sometimes called 'glocalisation', will last as long as the human race exists. There are times for heavy central control, for example during turnarounds from a crisis or for long term decisions, and there are times for delegation and localism, conventionally thought to be best during stable and expansionist times and where scale is less important and decisions are more short term – but also in chaotic fast changing situations when it's impossible for the centre to keep up with what's happening and provide timely direction.

The military concept of 'mission command' is one approach to reconciling the tensions, particularly adapted to chaotic situations[13]. It involves letting the front line know what you want to achieve, and then letting them get on with it, using their initiative to adapt to circumstances with no need to refer back for unforeseen problems. But it also involves establishing shared culture and values through training and standardised procedures, so that the individual actions of small teams tend to reinforce each other rather than cancel each other out.

In our view, the quality and speed of decisions made and the wisdom of the leadership usually matter more than the organisational structure. Small countries can be agile. They can make decisions quickly. They can also change direction and implement decisions quickly. Because they tend to be less self-sufficient and more interconnected and outward looking, they can sense and respond to new trends and changes in the world before the cumbersome bureaucracies of big countries even notice[14]. In principle, Scotland has all these advantages. Speed of decision-making and quality of leadership are, in our opinion, a key part of Scotland's success for the future and will be dealt with in future publications.

The Airport Boss

On the 7th of March 2038, the Chief Executive of the new Scottish airport, Alison O'Neill, sat down, exhausted, on the couch in her flat in central Stirling. It was an old building, sensitively and very expensively brought up to modern standards of insulation and connectivity. "Mum!" she called. Her home audio system discreetly started making the connection to her parents in Barnet, north London. This was the first opportunity to call them, late on a Sunday evening after an exhausting week.

On Thursday, she had completed the merger of the existing Edinburgh and Glasgow Airports into the new Scotland Central Airport. As befits the information age, the decisive moment, the point when it all seemed real at last, was when new three-letter airport identifier SCA replaced the old EDI and GLA identifiers in the international air traffic information system.

The "new" airport was built around the existing Edinburgh one, using most of the existing infrastructure; but with a brand new futuristic zero-carbon terminal and ground transport interchange, made entirely from home-grown Scottish timber, on the west side of the airport. This allowed much better ground transport connections throughout the central belt and beyond. The surveys were complete, the land reserved, and planning approvals obtained for a second runway, should it be required.

There had been a huge extended row about where to put the investment. That was resolved before she was appointed, thank goodness. She couldn't decide what had been the most difficult part of the saga for her. Was it fighting the hard-line Greens who had tried to prevent the first turf being cut in 2030? The debate about whether this actually reduced carbon footprint had raged on for 10 years ahead of the decision, and there still wasn't a clear answer. Or did she find more difficulty with the political ructions caused by the decision on what to do with the legacy Glasgow site – parkland, housing, Disneyworld, rewilding, recreational lakes? "A nightmare of inhabitants, lobbyists, and politicians!" Or was it just because, as a young, intelligent, forceful, Irish woman, she challenged the residues of last century's toxic central belt business culture – parochial, sectarian, older, male – in so many ways all at once?

Regardless, for better or worse the decision had finally been made. It was seen as a major part of the whole modernisation of transport infrastructure recommended by the Dutch-inspired study conducted in 2025 and re-examined in 2027. The superfast train from Glasgow Central directly to the terminal had swung it, she thought.

The phone call connected. "Hi Mum! Hi Dad! Good to hear you! How are you?"

"Oh, you know, the usual – how's your week been? We saw you on Thursday, a ten-second clip on the main BBC News. Presumably you got more airtime in Scotland?"

"Oh, yes, unfortunately. I hate seeing myself on screen. It's been a horrendous week, but I got through it. And, thank God and touch wood, we haven't had anything like the major glitches when Heathrow's Terminal 5 opened 40 years ago."

"Was it worth it, dear?" her mother asked sympathetically.

"What do you mean – is the new airport worth it, or for me personally?"

"Both," she replied.

"Well yes, otherwise it would never have passed the Scottish Government's scrutiny. It will cut numerous indirect flights to Scotland via Manchester, Gatwick, Heathrow, hmm… Stansted, Amsterdam… and even Dublin. Put Scotland on the map. Better connections to the North of Europe. Compete with Dublin now. Probably taken 5 years off my life, mind you!"

"Sorry to hear that dear," empathised her mother again.

Her father chipped in. "But your generation has always believed the environment is really important. I keep reading that aviation is still damaging us. Your cousins all complain about you being in it. They remind me of the ice melting… I feel so sorry for you."

"I'm used to that Dad," Alison reassured him, "So don't worry. You always said I was the toughest of your three daughters. I knew when I relocated to Scotland that this one was going to be a toughie. At least the new Scottish government has upped the carbon tax on aviation and gas guzzlers again. Most of the domestic flights are electric or hydrogen-powered, and we're the hub for the complete decarbonisation of the Scottish domestic network. Boris's new airport in the South of England helped. And oh, did you hear, Scottish domestic aviation reached carbon neutral this year, ahead of target. We would never have had a hope in hell without all of that!"

"Yes, I heard that. I also saw the major lobbying campaign by some people in Glasgow who were bitterly opposed to the closure of the Glasgow airport. I thought that East-West divide had gone away," added her Dad.

"No, there are still pockets that believe that Edinburgh, the capital, favours the east of the country and would rather drag everything over in that direction. At least the massive new marine engineering centre in the Clyde has given a bit more balance. It's prevented it looking too one-sided. Shame Scotland didn't decide in the 1930s when it was first studied. They should have picked Airth, the truly optimal site in the first place. Too late. Lesson learned, I guess, for the future. The cost of parochialism. A bit of a Scottish thing really.

"Sorry, Mum and Dad, it's been so good talking to you; but I'm really tired now, need to get going."

"OK, we'll let you go and get your beauty sleep. It's late. Are you still able to come down to see us next month?"

"Yes, still planning to take a few days break down south with you. No need to pick me up, I'll get the driverless Uber from the station. Don't tell anyone, but I'm planning to come by train!"

She slumped on her bed. "At least some people don't challenge me all the time," she muttered to herself.

University Challenge

Consolidate the universities to create world-class, world-scale centres of excellence

The Chancellor of the International Caledonian University (ICU), Sir Tim Ormand, took a few moments off from his overly busy schedule and cross-Scotland train journeys to pen a message to his peers in Harvard, Stanford, Cambridge, and Tsinghua Universities. The last of the fountain pen letter writers!

The Scottish universities had done well during the early 2020's but were finding it increasingly difficult to keep their high rankings in the world league table and expand their funding further. In 2025, the University of Edinburgh and Heriot Watt University had decided to merge, to be better able to capture international funding and expand their international network. In 2028, the three North-East Universities of Aberdeen, Robert Gordon's (also in the city of Aberdeen), and Dundee had followed suit. In 2030, Glasgow, Strathclyde, and

Glasgow Caledonian universities had completed their merger to form the controversially named International Caledonian University (ICU). In 2034, the University of St Andrews had decided finally, after a turbulent and agonised debate, to take the plunge and combine with the already integrated Aberdeen and Dundee Universities – particularly galling to the St Andrews traditionalists as Dundee had originally been a mere satellite of St Andrews, until it became independent in 1967.

Meanwhile the Scottish Government had finally driven all the Scottish Universities, with much resistance, to consolidate the various Management and MBA programmes into a single Leadership Campus near Stirling. An attempt to emulate the European's leading business school, INSEAD, set in the wooded forests of Fontainebleau outside Paris. A differentiation from the pure city location of the London Business School that was tied to the City of London financial services industry. Less controversially, the University of the Highlands and Islands had been revamped as the national University for the Environment (Agriculture, Marine, Biodiversity, and Forestry) headquartered in Inverness, with campuses throughout the Highlands and Islands, notably in Orkney and Shetland. The further education sector and the more vocational and practical university departments had been totally reorganised into a single national body tasked to deliver the best possible technical and vocational training, its organisation and ethos modelled on the fantastic Technical Schools which contribute so much to the German economy.

By 2034, those moves had given Scotland three large, broad-based Universities from eight sub-scale ones and a further two highly specialized academic institutions; and finally restored technical and vocational training to its rightful place alongside, rather than subordinate to, academic education. But for the top researchers, this was still too fragmented to attract world-scale international funding and high-quality students in the 2040s and beyond.

Sir Tim wrote with his favourite fountain pen flowing effortlessly across the luxurious bond paper.

My fellow international Chancellors,

You will read next month that we and the Scottish Government have concluded the negotiations to create an even larger University in Scotland, combining my International Caledonian University with Edinburgh-Heriot-Watt.

I told you over dinner at the Global University Summit in Shanghai two years ago that the merger of Glasgow and Strathclyde had taken 5 years to achieve and with real pain for many. Another five years on, it is time to take a further major step forward.

The much-expanded Scottish Research budget requires greater coordination for the future. We are very proud to be into our second decade of very high growth, with Russia, Norway, Sweden, Vietnam, Brazil, and Chile providing a fresh impetus, on top of the high levels of funding we have secured from China and India over the last two decades.

As you can imagine, we had a major question as to how to rename the University. The three-part name, Edinburgh Heriot Watt, was already too much of a mouthful, and our own name change to the International Caledonian University was an unsatisfactory compromise we always recognised as temporary. We will now abandon the legacy altogether and eliminate the East/West rivalry once and for all. It is time to move on from the wonderful names of the ancient Scottish universities, St Andrews, Glasgow, Aberdeen, and Edinburgh, that have had such longstanding academic brand value – 600 years from 1413 onwards – and that have served us so well in the past. Now we look to the future, with our proud new name, the Scottish Global University (SGU). The rationale is to allow greater scale in each University discipline and create a much larger new technology investment programme for Artificial Intelligence, Informatics, and the Fifth Industrial revolution. We are also taking the bold step of merging our very lucrative existing Management and MBA programmes into a single international leadership campus near Stirling.

I would be delighted to see you all again soon, once I settle into a new routine and before I retire in eighteen months' time to make way for my successor. Perhaps you could grace our shores during the official launch at Holyrood Palace on Burns Night early next year? We are proud of our achievements, and look forward to great success in the future, and to even stronger and more productive collaborations with your institutions.

Best wishes, Yours Aye

Sir Tim

Future Chancellor, The Scottish Global University

Visions of a smart carbon-neutral Scotland in 2070

Are Extinction Rebellion right? Do we need to crash the economy to tackle the climate crisis? Maybe not. If mankind makes the right decisions, we should be able to live in comfort in a low-carbon world. It will involve big lifestyle changes, certainly, but not necessarily for the worse – maybe even for the better.

Let's imagine we're visiting a carbon-neutral Scotland in 2070.

***

Our take-off from Schiphol airport in Holland is a strange experience. The hydrogen-powered boost trolley accelerates us quickly along the runway to the take-off speed of 130 knots without depleting the plane's batteries. There is a slight wobble as we separate from the boost trolley and float into the air. We climb gently and almost silently towards our cruising height, turning smoothly onto the most efficient course towards Edinburgh. The course is worked out by computer magic, allowing for forecast winds along the route and all the other planes using the same airspace.

Crossing the Dutch coast, we can appreciate for the first time the scale and ambition of the massive engineering works to upgrade the sea defences. The machinery and piles of material stretch as far as the eye could see in both directions, fading into the haze on the distant horizon. Rising sea levels are now an existential threat to Holland. Without this second massive upgrade to the sea defences, Schiphol would soon disappear under the waves.

Even with the plane dawdling at a frugal 360 knots, the flight time is the same as in 2020 thanks to the optimised routeing. We waste no time hanging around waiting for clearance to land – the computerised flight plans seamlessly interleave the arriving and departing planes. As we approach and land, most of the energy used to climb is recovered. The e-fan motors generate power as they slow us down, augmented on the ground by regenerative braking in the undercarriage. We are still braking hard as we whizz onto the angled exit ramp in a gentle high-speed turn. Getting off the runway more quickly saves precious seconds for each of the planes landing and taking off behind us. This and many other subtle changes and tweaks, each small by itself, increased runway capacity by nearly fifty percent. As a result, Edinburgh Airport was able to take over Glasgow's traffic when the Clyde threatened to flood the low-lying Abbotsinch Airport. Sea levels are now rising much faster than the worst predictions of fifty years ago, and Glasgow's runway is only a few metres above the 2020 sea level.

Scots' air travel became very different after the Covid-19 crisis. Business travel reduced significantly once firms discovered that they really could do much more of their business over the internet. More Scots holidayed at home as the climate became more pleasant, the British railway system was transformed, popular foreign holiday destinations were less attractive due to climate change and biodiversity loss, the carbon tax made long-haul air travel much more expensive, and well-timed low-carbon investments brought rapid economic growth. Edinburgh Airport was able to delay its plans for a second runway until the system architecture for zero-carbon civil aviation was settled, and the business case was clear. Air travel is now dominated by super-efficient medium-range electric planes (the competition between battery power and hydrogen fuel cells continues unabated). Long-haul travel is no longer point to point, except for the super-rich, but by a series of hops between hubs a couple of thousand miles apart. Transfers are really slick: modern technology makes queues for check-in, passport control, security and customs a distant folk memory. Now, if you dare, you can arrive at the airport ten minutes before the scheduled departure and not miss your flight. Ticket prices are dropping again. Edinburgh's ambition to become a key link in the air route from Eurasia to North America means that work on the second runway now proceeds apace. Fortuitously, the delayed decision let the airport take advantage of the very latest technology, doing away with the need for hydrogen boost trolleys and using the now-perfected carbon-absorbing concrete.

Because everyone on our plane cleared Scottish immigration and customs and biosecurity checks before take-off or in-flight, our onward connection is as easy as getting off a bus – in fact easier because of the automated baggage handling. The first-class passengers are picked up from the bottom of the steps, along with their bags, by autonomous hover-taxis. We walk off the plane and straight through the terminal to the auto-pod four-seat electric taxi that we'd booked when we were over the North Sea. We could have got the train all the way to our destination, but we are curious to sample this new mode of travel. Our bags arrive at the auto-pod at the same time as us, gliding silently behind us on a self-driving baggage truck. We set off in the autopod within five minutes of touching down, and we'll reach Glasgow by the time we'd have got through customs 50 years ago.

The autopod chooses the northern route to Glasgow, along the old M9 motorway. Motorways are now reserved for autonomous vehicles, which drive so much faster and closer together than human drivers that it's not safe for both to share the same road space. Our pod joins the back of a "platoon," about twenty vehicles so close together they slip-stream each other to save power. The driving processor in the lead vehicle sends its commands to all the vehicles in the platoon, so that if necessary, they all slow down together – no delays due to driver reaction time. Every now and then the platoons reorganise themselves. Each vehicle takes a turn at the front to share out the power-saving benefit.

Now we're passing the landfill site near Polmont. No more nasty smell – instead, a shiny biogas recovery structure collects the gas and burns it, feeding electricity to the power grid and capturing carbon dioxide to the Carbon Capture and Storage manifold a few kilometres away at Grangemouth. The flares from the Grangemouth refineries and chemical plants are also no more, the smell now sweet. All the methane is recovered from the high-value chemical processes and either burnt for electricity or chemically reformed into hydrogen or ammonia. The waste carbon dioxide is compressed to ninety atmospheres and pumped hundreds of miles into geological formations under the North Sea. In the 2020s, the Scottish Government resisted calls from the Committee on Climate Change to commit to the unproven BECCS (Bio Energy Carbon Capture and Storage) fad. If Scotland had gone that way, the available CCS capacity would be used up by now, huge areas of landscape would be ruined by quick-growing monocultures frequently harvested, and our industry would have nowhere to put its unavoidable carbon emissions. As it is, Scotland still has plenty of CCS capacity. It is coining money from Carbon Credits, and also from the industries that most countries had to abandon because of their carbon emissions. These industries came to Scotland to use the CCS capacity to capture the emissions from their current manufacturing processes. They stayed to work with Scottish universities and research centres to develop the next generation processes that will get rid of the carbon emissions altogether.

Past Grangemouth, the low-lying farmland to the right of the motorway succumbed to the rising sea level and is now salt marsh. Economically unproductive, it's a treasure of biodiversity, a complete complex ecosystem of a type that used to be common in Europe and is now rare. While welcoming this in principle, SEPA (the Scottish Environmental Protection

Agency) keeps an intense watch, bordering on the paranoid, for any hint that the warming climate and extended marshland might be attracting malarial mosquitos.

To the left of the road, Falkirk and Stenhousemuir look radically different from fifty years ago. Since the 2020s, all new-build houses in Scotland have been engineered to the German Passiv Haus standard – zero emission, and so well insulated and aired that for much of the year the heat generated by the occupants and electrical appliances is enough to keep the place warm. The houses were all built of locally sourced wood – a challenge in the early years, before the massive planting programme caught up with demand. A huge programme to retrofit external insulation and better draught proofing and ventilation to existing houses transformed both their appearance and their year-round comfort, while drastically reducing heating bills and carbon emissions. Demand for gas collapsed – hardly anyone in Scotland uses it for home heating or cooking any more. England took a very different approach – prioritising expensive electricity-powered heat pumps to heat the houses, along with more modest improvements in insulation, instead of solving the problem at source by removing the need to heat the houses in the first place[15].

Because much less energy is now used for home heating, Scotland has plenty of generating capacity to charge batteries and make hydrogen for aeroplanes and ammonia for ships. This makes it, along with Iceland, a hugely attractive hub for zero-emission aviation and sea traffic, because the energy surplus allows the airports and ports to offer cheaper refuelling costs than most of their competitors.

Between Denny and Cumbernauld, we cross the line of the new Hyperloop transit system from Glasgow to Perth, Aberdeen, and Inverness. Again, the land has changed since 2020. Instead of large green fields and dark solid blocks of forest, trees are everywhere, at varying density. Grazing animals move among the trees, most of them kept close together in the "mob grazing" method that improves the health of the soil and encourages trees to regenerate naturally. A bewildering range of vegetables grows in small lush plots and greenhouses among the trees. Some of the older trees are being harvested – not big areas clear-felled all at once, but selected trees plucked out from among the continuous woodland. In late November, the landscape is still green, though leaves are starting to turn brown in the crisp fresh autumnal air. A month before Christmas, the weather is like it was in late

September in 2020. Strange southern tree species flourish. Some of the old native species are declining, only surviving further north and higher up the hillsides.

As we head down the M80 and approach Glasgow, the platoon of autopods moves into the inside lane, slows to a hundred kilometres an hour, and starts to separate. Vehicles peel off. Ours drops us at Springburn, and a few minutes later we board a train for Milngavie. It's smooth! It's comfortable! It's clean! It's quick! It connects with a bus at the other end which takes us to our final destination, dropping us at the door. Gosh, how Glasgow has changed. Free integrated public transport in the Greater Glasgow area, and the convenience of autopods, means that hardly anyone has a car anymore. The trains and buses, now run by the Greater Glasgow Community Trust, are so good and so dependable that Scotland now meets the definition of a developed country – not a place where the poor own cars, but one where the rich use public transport[16]. The downside of this is that Edinburgh Airport had to abandon its plan to use holiday-makers' cars parked for two weeks as a huge battery bank for refuelling aircraft – there are not enough privately-owned cars to make it work. Most of the car parks have been turned into solar farms.

Our hosts' house is cool without being cold, fresh and airy without being draughty. "Solar panels heat the water and provide some electricity," they explain "When we need more, it's imported from the grid. When we generate surplus, we export it to the grid if the price is right, otherwise it gets stored in the house battery or hot water tank." The house is smaller than professional middle-class people would have owned fifty years ago. Taking a lead from Scandinavia and Germany, houses are now valued as homes, not investments, and waste and ostentation are gently frowned upon in most social circles. Small, modular, factory-built houses and low-rise apartment blocks, with excellent heat and sound insulation, private allotments and well-maintained safe public spaces made houses affordable again and encouraged people to live nearer their work. Because hardly anyone owns a car, there are no garages or drives. Most people walk or cycle to work, or they use the free public transport. The section of the old M8 between Newhouse and central Glasgow is a linear public park, with flourishing trees and bushes and numerous bird species[17]. Pine martens drove away the grey squirrels, and native red squirrels are a common sight again in Glasgow's parks.

Batteries and hydrogen fuel cells continued to drop spectacularly in price and improve in performance in the 2020s and '30s, banishing the worries about intermittency in renewable energy. Utility companies bought massive battery banks, and smart demand management lets you choose whether you want power all the time for whatever you've switched on at whatever the cost, or whether you want to save money by turning things off when the price is higher because there's not enough wind or too much demand. Excess power is used to produce hydrogen which has replaced liquid fuel in most applications that can't be satisfied by electricity. Massive investment in tidal turbines in the 20s and 30s provided enough baseload to replace the old nuclear power plants at Hunterston and Torness when they were phased out. Scottish tidal turbines are now sold all over the world, wherever there are tides strong enough to generate useful power. The power grids across the British Isles and near-Europe are all inter-connected to make sure there are no black-outs if any one area is short of wind or solar power. The English nuclear reactors were replaced with new generation small modular reactors (SMRs) in the 2030s – British industry got its act together on these only just in time to avoid losing out yet again to the Americans. British SMR's are in widespread use across many countries – not Scotland, though, because the Scottish Government maintained its passionate opposition to nuclear power in any form.

Other changes since 2020 have been more incremental. The archaic three-bladed wind turbines are being replaced with solid state ones with no moving parts – far cheaper and more reliable, and a good source of export earnings. Wave power efforts were abandoned – too hard, and other forms of renewable energy were proving easier and more profitable. Hydro power also didn't make the comeback some expected. The easy half of Scotland's hydro potential was already exploited. The remaining capacity would be more expensive, the concrete in hydro dams caused a lot of carbon emission before there was any payback, and the land they occupied was more valuable for combined agriculture and forestry. The tidal turbine technology transferred easily to run-of-the-river hydro in fast flowing rivers, which made a useful but not decisive contribution to the country's energy needs.

All in all, Scotland is now a net carbon absorber across its whole economy. The huge transformation was funded by the last years of oil revenue and by patient money in pension funds, which were looking for long-term investments offering steady and sustainable returns.

There is one fly in the ointment, a shadow on the future horizon. Nuclear fusion has long been the holy grail of abundant "free" energy. Ever since the idea was first floated in the 1950s, right through to the 2040s, commercial fusion power has always been 'thirty years away.' The hugely ambitious and deeply troubled British fusion power project that started in 2020 is now finally bearing fruit. England expects to be self-sufficient in energy thanks to its fusion power programme within twenty years. Every other country in the world is now having to reappraise its energy strategy in light of this.

"What do you think of it all, then?" our friends ask us as we help them tidy away after dinner – a salmon dish with a wonderful concoction of exotic vegetables, fruit and seeds, all grown by regenerative agriculture businesses within fifty miles of Glasgow, settled with a fine malt whisky. Some things have stayed just the same as 50 years ago, for very good reason!

"The meal? Absolutely delicious, thanks."

"Oh, thank you – but I meant coming back to Scotland after fifty years away."

"Oh, everything looks fantastic. What a transformation! Clean, industrious, prosperous, modern, healthy people, and a healthy environment. Who'd have thought it fifty years ago? Scotland 2070 – healthy, wealthy and wise!"

***

"You can't be serious!" we hear some of you shout, emulating the famous rant by John McEnroe at the line judges during the Wimbledon Tennis Championships when a marginal line call was judged either in or out. "That was definitely out! Over the line. Too idyllic, idealistic, unrealistic, even impossible!"

Well, let's look at the replay a few times to check.

Too idyllic? Maybe. Don't discount the hard work and amount of change involved to get there; and would life really be idyllic with all these new information technologies invading our privacy?

Possible? Yes it is. All but one of the technologies and the knowledge needed to create that future already exist, and most are proven at scale. The exception - no-one yet has a plausible concept for grid-scale wind generators with no moving parts. But ideas are being tried out, and who knows where that might get to in fifty years.

Realistic? Even the replay is not quite clear. That's down to us. If we sit around waiting for it to happen to us, it won't. If we want it, are willing to commit to the vision, and work to make it happen, why not? It would need leadership, money, and resources - like everything else we've discussed in this book. The resources we mostly have. Leadership and money are questions we discuss in the final chapter, and intend to come back to in future work.

References for Chapter 7

[1] UK Infrastructure and Projects Authority, Analysis of the National Infrastructure and Construction Pipeline, 2018

[2] ibid.; Institute for Public Policy Research, Transport Investment In The Northern Powerhouse 2019 update; Scottish Government, Infrastructure Investment Plan 2015: progress report 2019 to 2020.

[3] Stern, Lord Nicholas, Towards a low-carbon future, lecture to Oxford Martin School, November 2017 - https://www.oxfordmartin.ox.ac.uk/downloads/events/171102_Stern_lecture.pdf

[4] https://www.theguardian.com/technology/2012/apr/15/estonia-ussr-shadow-internet-titan?CMP=Share_iOSApp_Other

[5] https://www.weforum.org/agenda/2020/07/estonia-advanced-digital-society-here-s-how-that-helped-it-during-covid-19/

[6] https://www.metsawood.com/global/news-media/videos/Pages/Mjosa-Tower-worlds-tallest-wood-building.aspx

[7] Logan M, 'Scottish Technology Ecosystem Review', Scottish Government, 25th August 2020

[8] Bettencourt and West, A Unified Theory of Urban Living, Nature 467, 912-13(2010) https://doi.org/10.1038/467912a https://www.nature.com/articles/467912a#citeas

[9] https://en.wikipedia.org/wiki/List_of_UK_cities_by_GVA

[10] Main Lever & Crook, Central Scotland Airport Study, David Hume Institute, 2003

[11] Locality Report, *Saving money by doing the right thing - Why 'local by default' must replace 'diseconomies of scale'.* Locality and Vanguard Consulting, 2014

[12] Lesley Riddoch, *Blossom*, Luath Press, (3rd edition) 2018

[13] https://en.wikipedia.org/wiki/Mission_command

[14] See (particularly Chapter 9) Michael O'Sullivan, The levelling: what's next after globalisation. PublicAffairs, June 2019

[15] This appears to be the approach indicated in the Future Homes Standard consultation issued in October 2019. https://www.gov.uk/government/consultations/the-future-homes-standard-changes-to-part-l-and-part-f-of-the-building-regulations-for-new-dwellings

[16] Former mayor of Bogotá Gustavo Petro, quoted by Ellie Harrison in The Glasgow Effect, Luath, 2019.

[17] Thanks to Ellie Harrison writing in "The Glasgow Effect" (Luath, 2019) for this idea!

Chapter 8

Winning in the New World

"Men and nations do act wisely when they have exhausted all the other possibilities."

Unattributed

"It is not the strongest of the species that survives, nor the most intelligent, but the one most responsive to change."

Charles Darwin

This book is our story about Scotland's future. It describes our vision for our grandchildren's home country in fifty years' time; and practical steps about how to get there from here.

The final chapter recapitulates and summarises the story of the six major global trends and market opportunities discussed in chapters 2 to 7. The opportunities are there. It's up to us to harness them to create the sustainable wealth that would allow Scotland and all its people to thrive in this world of change.

Scotland winning: the six big opportunities

Take Advantage of The Melting Ice

Our story starts with the now-inevitable melting of the Arctic sea ice. This will be one of the most significant global changes to affect world trade since the Suez and Panama Canals opened. Within 25 years, Scotland will be on the doorstep of a major new global trading passage and a new economic region in the Arctic. This small country on the periphery of Europe will be presented with all sorts of new market opportunities, thanks to large-scale growth in East/West trade flows across the top of Russia and the investment in the region. Scotland will stop looking South, and face North instead.

Use the Land More Effectively

The second part of our story is the enrichment of the land, and its more imaginative and productive use for the benefit of all. Scotland can, if it really chooses, reforest a large swathe of the countryside on a scale never planned for before. Imagine five billion more trees in Scotland, a mix of commercial forestry and wild foresting – mixed natural and biodiverse woodland interspersed with fertile glades and well-maintained paths. Imagine the impact on the climate change agenda, on the economy, on rural jobs, and on Scotland's reputation for being a country ready to change. Imagine introduction of the best new agricultural methods – highly productive farming techniques that take carbon out of the atmosphere, instead of putting more in. It is a tangible and realistic opportunity, if we have the will, to transform our countryside – though it does seem to involve tackling significant vested interests, traditional methods and preconceptions.

A Transition to Renewables

We continue with Scotland's underutilised land, sea, rivers, and wind. If managed well, these can transform the country into a major exporter of renewable energy and technology. Wind and tidal are the obvious targets: these are energy sources that can often produce more electricity than is required to meet consumers' need. This excess, that would otherwise be wasted, can be used to produce hydrogen – another form of green energy – from water. Unlike some less fortunate countries with limited resources, we can use our remaining oil and gas to fund such an exciting expansion and transition over the next 50 years. This is all part of the potential for the 'natural economy', which is now recognised as a key part of a country's assets – in Scotland's case estimated as being worth over £29bn per year[1].

Pursue Healthcare Ambitiously

We then move on to medicine. The entire healthcare and medical world, already challenged on multiple fronts, is now reeling from the Covid-19 crisis. The Brain is the new focus after 50 years of astounding progress on the Heart. Brain health is seen to be central to many aspects of future healthcare. A revamping of Primary Care and Public Health is also called for. Telemedicine; simpler testing; and new, better, and flexible frontline services are seen to be essential for both mental health and to tackle the major physical illnesses such as cancer. Automation of the healthcare sector will accelerate exponentially, representing a revolution in the UK's care industry to deal with an ageing population and serve the 'silver economy'. Medical security of supply is as important now as military and energy security of supply.

Scotland starts from a solid albeit not perfect base: renowned medical research; appropriate medical venture capital; a stable healthcare system; and an ageing population to serve. Since Scotland has a good position in the sector and only a few opportunities for sustained economic growth in other sectors, it is essential that Scotland invests in, and makes money from, successful healthcare and life sciences businesses that supply the growing NHS needs. Otherwise, the insatiable demand and inflation from the ageing population and its social issues will consume its overall wealth and pass that wealth to other countries.

Double Research, Triple Development and re-orientate Industrial policy

Our fifth vision is the toughest to realise: transform Scotland's industrial policy. Look to our European neighbours: successful small countries that are serious about innovation. For too long, Scotland has relied on inspiration from England, Germany, Silicon Valley, and Japan on how to run a country and its industrial policy. We have much to learn from the wealthier and happier, similar-sized Nordic countries. Investment in innovation, different land use, devolved Government, engaged communities, social policy, and hard, focused work ethic. It's time to effect a change in perspective.

We can reverse our over-dependence on Financial Services, and avoid the trap of competing with Ireland, with their low corporate tax, low R&D spend, and a fiercely loyal diaspora. On the contrary, we should double our funds for R&D in Scottish Universities, research centres, and innovative companies; and triple the development investment in Scotland's potential strengths in medical, maritime, renewable energy, and AI-based markets.

We hear you say, "but how can we afford this?" One option is to wrench Scotland away from the UK's delusion of being a global superpower. Refuse to contribute to infrastructure spend that has no material benefit to Scotland, and learn from the failed attempt to create sustainable manufacturing jobs in the Silicon Glen era of the 1980s. Another option is to fight for a Keynesian injection of R&D spend as part of a post-Covid stimulus. There may even be a third, if we could convince our rich neighbouring country, Norway, to invest in Scotland's future as a diversification from its own economy.

Reform Infrastructure

For our final suggestions, we recognise that Scotland's infrastructure is in desperate need of reform. Transport can be rebuilt around electric aircraft networks, Dutch-inspired network thinking, super-fast broadband, and the elimination of East/West parochial behaviours. In fact, Scotland is such a small country that it ought to pursue the creation of a 'Virtual City State of five million people.' Virtual inter-connectedness is desperately needed for a radical change of working practices. Successful, but smaller-scale Universities and institutions can be consolidated to compete more strongly in the new world order. Radical new housing techniques and regulations can create a wood-based and environmentally friendly future for infrastructure.

Scotland's Future – A 50-Year Journey

"Success is not final, failure is not fatal: it is the courage to continue that counts."

Winston Churchill

Five years, or even twenty, is too short a timeframe for a national vision. We prefer the perspective of a UK Foreign Office private briefing on China: words to the effect, *China was the number one economy in the world for sixteen of the last eighteen centuries. China fumbled the ball for 200 years because of a lack of attention to military technology, an inward-looking phase and a less than successful experiment with not relying on capitalism. However, it's on its way back to the top by 2040, now that it's got its act together, reversed its introversion, adopted capitalism and invested in large-scale manufacturing using its vast population.* That's a much better timeframe for a vision in the context of history, albeit a stretch too far for most people worried about putting food on the table for the next year, or month even. So, we have chosen a fifty-year view as a realistic timeframe to change a country, the appropriate timeframe for our and the next two generations.

In order to achieve our vision, we have to free up our minds. A robust vision can cope with failures along the way. Compromises will be made, and tactics altered. Take the 30-year vision of Morita, the brilliant founder of Sony: he described it in person to one of the authors during a Stanford Business School lecture in 1979 by explaining, *I wanted to help change the image of Japan in the eyes of the world. In 1946, Japan had just been defeated and I was keen to help restore Japan to a triumphant nation once again. While everyone in America wanted bigger and better products, I wanted to miniaturise the large US tape recorders donated to the Japanese school rooms in the 1940s, make them suitable for Japan's small spaces, and eventually to fit into your own pocket.* Of course, Morita experienced many disappointments and failures, requiring changes in tactics. However, he never lost sight of the overall vision, and achieved it with the Sony Walkman in 1979, over thirty years after his vision was first formed. He even designed a shirt for American salesmen with a bigger pocket so that they could demonstrate the success a little earlier.

Our own vision for Scotland is not about who is in charge for the next five or ten years. It is not a linear strategy, at risk of failing at the first setback. It's not all or nothing. There will be disappointments and changes and mistakes and unexpected successes along the way. The

198

untold story of Scotland's winning future cannot be constrained by the bald binary framing of 'No' versus 'Yes.' No-one knows what that really means anyway. It cannot be constrained by phrases such as 'Home Rule' or 'Federalism' or 'Abolishing Devolution.' None of these are inspiring destinations, as the last three years of Brexit have shown. Our story should largely survive the issue of whether Scotland becomes an independent country or not.

In fact, we believe that our vision will survive even if we can't get the best compromise between the Greens' opposition to the current economic growth model, and the oilmen's continued promotion of investment in fossil fuels. Maybe wind energy will turn out not to be the best way for future renewables. Maybe we will run out of the rare earth resources required for so-called renewables. Maybe new sources of investment funds will have to be found, outside of Britain's traditionally narrow scope.

But the only true force capable of killing our vision is the continuation of a state of fear: a fear of Brexit; a fear of Covid-19; a fear of climate change; a fear of further automation; a fear of the SNP, or the currency; a media-sponsored doom and gloom; a fear of further change; and the sometimes heard statements of being too small, too poor, and too stupid. An echo of Private Fraser's famous phrase in Dad's Army – "We're Doomed!"

Scotland's Future – A Winning Trilogy – Two more steps

Scotland is certainly 'doomed' in one way. Small countries can't do everything – they are 'doomed to choose[2]' – and, having chosen, to take responsibility for their choices. We believe strongly that there are a few significant opportunities for Scotland to win in the new world and create sustainable wealth. We think that is within our grasp, and we invite you to step into that vision in this book. But the next debate we wish to sponsor concerns two further major steps in the journey beyond understanding how to create sustainable wealth: what leadership is required; and how can this ambition be funded?

What Leadership is Required?

"I start with the premise that the function of leadership is to produce more leaders, not more followers." – Ralph Nader

The Lost Leaders

Over 200 years ago, Samuel Johnson said "Sir, the noblest prospect that a Scotchman ever sees, is the high road that leads him to London." Many of our best and brightest still head south for greater challenge and career opportunity. Our vision and deep desire is to reverse that traffic, to make Scotland the best place to live and work in the British Isles.

The flow of Scottish talent to London and abroad benefitted us during the empire era, as trade and commerce flowed back to Scotland. Now the economic return from the empire has dried up; but the loss of home grown talent continues.

Throughout their own lives, the authors have heard the older generation say "It's too late to rebuild. The country has been drained of leadership beyond the point of no-return." This pessimism stems not from false nostalgia and aging, but from a genuine fear that we can no longer reverse the trend. The loss certainly started a long time ago. Scots have always been emigrants and adventurers. Scottish merchants went all over Europe, and Scottish mercenaries fought in European wars, throughout the late middle ages. The drain was redirected to London at the beginning of the Union, and then towards the colonies, and has never stopped since. The loss was amplified by the Highland Clearances in the 19th Century, and by the devastating deaths during the two World Wars. But some believe the last 40 years have been the worst.

Perhaps this is not surprising in the context of what has been happening throughout Britain.

One of the authors spent much of his life based in London, building and selling excellent small British engineering companies to non-British corporations. He sold an industrial consulting business that he established to the Germans. He turned around and then sold a successful world class UK publicly-traded, oil and gas software company to the

Japanese, who beat American and German suitors - not a UK buyer in sight! He also helped to sell an English based high-tech company to the USA, and a share of Airbus to the French and Germans. Sadly, he was not able to save a failing Scottish company that had fallen on very bad times in the era of austerity and severe Government cutbacks.

Britain is bad enough at sustaining successful new companies able to compete in the global scene. Scotland is perhaps worse. Too often, promising start-ups are sold overseas for a quick return. We have not found the Scandinavians' capacity to create large and globally competitive corporations, outside of Financial Services. The one potential global corporation that could have been created from the oil industry, the British National Oil Company based in Glasgow, was sold early rather than being built in the same fashion as Norway created the highly successful, state-owned Equinor, previously called Statoil (State-Oil).

Our talented young folk are still seduced by greater opportunities in London and beyond. They won't be attracted back by a simple plea to return. They will only return if they believe that there is something exciting to build and lead, and a better quality of life for them and their families. In our view, the trigger for the return of a spirit of leadership is not simply from constitutional change, although that might assist. Rather, we think it will come largely from the (re)creation of long-term sustainable wealth-creating economic activity in Scotland – new businesses, ideally home-grown, and ideally remaining Scottish-owned and Scottish-based. (This is a chicken and egg argument, of course; to attract and foster leadership talent, we need the prospect of a secure economic future; to create a secure economic future, we need leadership talent!)

How Scotland reverses this trend deserves a book in itself. Gordon Brown's book provides an excellent diagnosis but is devoid of solutions. The story of another author gives a clue as to what is needed. He spent his early career with the great engineering company known at the time as Ferranti Scotland. It was set up in 1942 in Edinburgh, away from the bombing, to make gyro gunsights for Spitfires. In its current incarnation of Leonardo, it is part of a successful world class world scale defence electronics company. In the 80s and 90s, you could hardly visit a high-tech start-up in eastern Scotland without bumping into Ferranti alumni. This one successful and enduring company, with its high throughput of skilled engineering technicians and professionals and managers, stimulated a whole industrial and commercial ecosystem.

The Leadership Priorities

It is evident from speaking to representatives from all six target sectors, that no part of this vision will be achieved without tackling Scotland's leadership deficit. Our priority therefore would be to attract back and develop indigenous leadership for the six sectors that we have identified as critical. The characteristics we would seek are those with an entrepreneurial spirit, willingness to develop the vision further, passion for Scotland's success, and some experience of both success and failure. The political, civil service, economic and academic leaders would need to be supportive of the vision and these leaders.

In future publications we will explore how to encourage leadership and leaders to emerge within Scotland. It is safe to assert, even at this stage, that we are seeking to develop future leaders with the ability to use factual knowledge and situational insight to act decisively at any given point; the necessary resolve to see action through; and the flexibility to adjust when thwarted by unforeseen circumstances or events.

Because there are no world-class leadership establishments within Scotland, many Scots who want to develop leadership skills beyond school and university also leave for institutions outside of Scotland, such as LSE and INSEAD, London Business School, Windsor Leadership College, the Aspen Initiative, and the excellent UK Government senior leadership institutions such as the Royal College for Defence Studies (RCDS) and the Civil Service National Leadership Centre. One possible solution to breed the next generation of senior leaders is to establish a world class Scottish Leadership Institute. This could emulate INSEAD that sits in the Fontainbleu forests, or be adapted from the Aspen Institute in Aspen, Colorado, to include specialized leadership training for Scotland's key focus areas. Many locations could be considered for such an institute. The authors like the idea of Stirling, a central location for the whole of Scotland, or near Gleneagles, to use an existing world-wide brand.

The leadership styles taught at such an Institution would, of course, be diverse. The professor at the Aspen Institute of Leadership in Colorado had seen many of the best US and International leaders pass through his institute. One of the authors asked him in the 1990s towards the end of a week-long crash course in leadership, what makes a good leader? His immediate answer was a surprise. "Anyone that can find a way to convince four mugs to follow them!" When challenged for a more practical and less flippant definition he continued, "There are a variety of successful leadership styles: fear, greed, servant-leadership, charisma, super energy and positional authority." He of course dismissed fear and greed as politically unacceptable to encourage in western democracies.

But leadership isn't just about the people at the very top. Leadership happens at every level. And leadership at the top is surely about the ability to create more leaders as Nader has pointed out. A football coach or a social worker or a nurse or a teacher is just as much in a leadership position, and has just as much leadership influence on those around them, as the CEO of a football club, or a senior civil servant or politician, or a hospital manager or a head teacher. Parental leadership is equally important. Here, we'll just say that leadership needs to be demonstrated and developed at every level of society and every level of every organisation. A grass roots revival in leadership aspiration and fortitude can assist a flagging nation.

Leadership development starts at an early age. Unfortunately yet inevitably, in mass school systems, conformity and academic success are usually the primary objectives. Often a few are picked out early as potential leaders based on very narrow criteria. The head boys and girls and prefects are typically conformists because they add structure and cause less disruption. But we all know leadership in society requires a wider skill and is certainly not about conformity – that's more to do with management skills than pure leadership. We also know that in many circles the academic A's end up working for the C's. Trying new things, taking risks, being prepared to be seen to be wrong, willingness to try and fail, and being bold, are often not the characteristics encouraged at school. However, these are the traits that often underpin leadership later. So, is the aspiration of creating Scottish leaders really built into the expectations of primary teachers, parents and social workers? Are headmasters or headmistresses really trying to create leaders, rather than simply focusing on academic success, competence and school conformity? Is each child in school given some leadership responsibility, however small?

We would certainly encourage more inspirational initiatives such as the one that BBC Scotland broadcast, a four-part series on the Arctic Academy. A group of ordinary kids, from Bathgate Academy, an ordinary school in central Scotland, were invited to participate in an extra-ordinary adventure – a full-on arctic exploration trip to Greenland. The message is simple: with a bit of help and encouragement, ordinary people can do extra-ordinary things. How do we give everyone in Scotland the opportunity to find out what they are really capable of?

Outside of schooling, the demise of institutions such as scouts and guides may have reduced the opportunity to learn responsibility for others at a young age. Perhaps the largescale reduction in the military and cadets had the same effect in teenage and adult life. Is there an alternative? Could clubs and community service programmes, run by teenagers themselves, replace some of those lost societal leadership training grounds? Or has the fear of abuse killed the goose that laid the leadership eggs.

In summary, what we envisage is the wholesale improvement in leadership and skills experienced in Ireland as a result of the remarkable achievements triggered by the senior civil servant, Thomas Kenneth Whitaker[3]. He was motivated by seeing the rampant emigration and lack of entrepreneurial spirit and the atmosphere of national despondency in the 1950s[4]. It is not an exaggeration to call him 'The Architect of Modern Ireland' after he published his transformational Economic Development in 1958[5]. The flood of talent that came back to Ireland and the new indigenous leadership created was remarkable to see, and caused a major turnaround in the country's fortunes.

A Shift in Mindset

Our vision will only happen if it can be sold positively to the Scottish people and they continue to believe in it for decades to come. A change of heart and mind is required to overcome the lack of risk-taking and fear of failure present in Scotland currently. Secondly, and equally importantly, strong institutions would be in place to ensure that politicians do not stray into their normal habit of seeking marginal votes or pandering to the vested interests that might block this vision. Strong steering committees, local think tanks, audit commissions, and civil servants are a precondition for steering this success.

We will address these issues of leadership in future publications. What type of leadership do we need? How do we attract the talent back and how do we create the entrepreneurial and ambitious talent within the country itself?

How Can this Ambition be Funded?

The new ambitious leadership will need funding. Do the Scottish people think that the major funding for this transition will flow naturally, because the prospects are so good; or are we still stuck with the belief that we have run out of money for the transformation required to capture the new world? That is a very important question, and one we want to address in future publications. We will discuss the demise of austerity, the rise of Modern Monetary Theory, and the Keynesian resurgence, and re-examine the options to reduce defence spending – and indeed what we would need to defend against – together with other relevant issues. Is our proposition attractive enough for Norway to invest big time? How about a Nordic alliance, with Norway's Sovereign Wealth Fund financing a "Viking Plan" to emulate the Marshall Plan?

As part of that question, we'll ask: do we have the confidence to make the hard choices, to work hard for this vision and make it real? Or are we unable to keep the bigger picture in view, beyond more immediate and tangible concerns such as currency, borders, passports, short term NHS funding, student fees, education decline, RBS headquarter location, politicians' personalities, to name but a few?

Scotland's Future – Our Belief and Vision

So why have we authors changed our minds about how best to achieve a thriving future for Scotland? Simple, really. Firstly, we have realised the long-term significance of the melting ice for Scotland's opportunities. Secondly, as we travelled, lived abroad, and reflected on the effects of different land ownership structures, we have realised the untapped potential from forestry and agriculture. Thirdly, we believe strongly that Scotland has the chance to use its remaining oil wealth to sponsor its transition to renewables and a research-based economy. Fourthly, we have great confidence in our medical strengths, marine culture, financial services quality, and further engineering prowess to 'double our R and triple our D' and win in the new technological world. And finally, the new digital age allows us to by-pass some of the investments in outdated infrastructure expenditure and shift to a more visionary investment in a virtual city state.

So here it is. Our vision for Scotland, post empire, post Brexit, and post Covid-19. A bold turnaround proposal. 50 years of hard work to reverse the effects of the globalisation and lack of investment that destroyed Scottish industry, and to build wealth from innovation during the current fourth industrial revolution.

Our Vision:

- **Look North for the next 100 years, not South;**
- **Steward our land, air, and sea resources much more effectively;**
- **Become again one of the world's most innovative nations.**

Our Strategy:

- **Invest in the new Arctic economic region and trade route ;**
- **Use the remaining years of oil profits to fund a substantial renewables export industry;**
- **Reforest the land and triple the wood-based economy;**
- **Invest in the medical and healthcare world to become a world leader in a few select areas, not simply a follower;**
- **Double Research and triple Development in selected sectors;**
- **Invest radically in a more cohesive infrastructure – a "Virtual City State" – and provide a market for the wood-based economy.**

The Scots, like any people facing these challenges, will find this to be a tough transition. More investment, less consumption. More collaboration within Scotland and with overseas partners so as to compete better in world markets. We will certainly have to use all the advantages known to be used by other successful small countries: easy and quick access to key decision-makers; faster decision-making; encouragement of less bureaucracy and hierarchy; a focus on doing a few things really well; adoption of singular and coherent country policies to establish strong international collaboration; and use of clear measures of performance.

We believe it is worthwhile – not only for ourselves, but particularly for our children and grandchildren.

The world has changed fundamentally. Let's imagine our task now as more of a post-war recovery plan and less as a series of incremental steps. Our vision is not about the constitution; it's about re-imagining Scotland as a thriving 21st-century nation. Disruptive

207

economist Mariana Mazzucato[6] would advise Scotland to think big and adopt a moon-shot mindset. In so doing, that other disruptive economist, Kate Raworth[7], would counsel us to see the big picture and create to regenerate – that is, to build a truly sustainable economy, that serves rather than dominates our society, and is regenerative by design.

Is there an alternative?

You may ask, "Are we missing anything to make a successful Scotland more likely or is there an alternative vision?"

From what we have experienced ourselves and seen in academic studies, a successful country must offer the world a few very special, not necessarily unique, attributes versus other competing nations. Scotland has used its educational excellence, geographical quaintness, scientific and engineering prowess and hard-working spirit, its proximity to London, combined with whisky brands and offshore oil, to give it an edge, at least in the past. America has offered the world vast mineral resources, high-volume farming, very lucrative support during the wealth-destroying European wars, financial risk-taking, an entrepreneurial spirit, and a Las Vegas, Hollywood, Disney, and Broadway culture that give it an edge over 70 years. England has used its naval might to rule the seas, financial acumen, and military skill to control large parts of the world, and scientific and educational prowess combined with superb civil servants and the backing of the Anglican church to punch well above its weight. Singapore has exploited its uniquely positioned deep water port, central to a massively growing trading region, and used its surrounding, low-cost labour as their special skills in the world. An excellent use of positional authority, you may say.

Our belief is that the six areas that we have highlighted provide the best shot at a successful Scotland in the next 50 years. Deep water oil, niche food and drink, financial services, and a multi-sector inward investment programme, although all good in themselves, will no longer be a sufficient basis for future success.

Fortunately, the six are not inter-dependent. Our ideas are based on a mix of geographical position, untapped local land and sea assets, a focus on two global trends (environment, and ageing populations), and a new set of relationships in the northern hemisphere. The vision is not based on a single silver bullet or a Las Vegas roll of the dice. The failure of one or two of these ideas does not jeopardise the whole vision.

In any case, it is highly risky to rely on one sector to be a nation's raison d'être. Saudi Arabia's wealth is a flash in the oil pan. That was derived from a 50-year golden era that is starting to unravel. They are desperately in need of a new vision and are perhaps expecting too much from their 2030 vision in too short a time frame. Japan had its forty-year boom until the late 1990s, sponsored mainly by the USA, focused on high-quality and miniature consumer goods, but is now in desperate need of a new vision also. Germany continues to benefit, post war, from modern industrial export prowess: machine tools; large consumer goods such as high-quality cars; and household goods feeding the world's rising wealthy class, currently in India, China, and the East. Will that last much longer? Some have their doubts. In the USA, oil, farming, and a growing local consumer market have been replaced, from the 1960s onwards, by a Government-sponsored Silicon Valley, an international defence export boom, and a burgeoning entertainment industry.

The latest Scottish Government's inward investment plan, published in October 2020[8], refocuses efforts to attract inward investment aligned to Scotland's 'values and priorities'. This is essential to start moving the economy in the right direction in the post Covid-19 era, but it's not enough for a 50-year success.

What might happen if we don't adopt a bold vision? We are in danger of looking at where the puck has been rather than where it is going, as the Canadian ice hockey icon would say. We believe that Scotland could easily default to dependency on three mature sectors. Financial services – a seductively attractive sector, but one that is increasingly automated and contributing further to the wealth divide – is in competition with growing European financial centres, and highly dependent on the rest of the Scottish economy for its success. Whisky has the risk of becoming a socially unacceptable product, like tobacco, and is already a very low-employment sector. And thirdly, tourism runs the risk of making us – together with a large number of other poor nations – overdependent on a sector which is already generally a low-value and low-wage one. We can't be reliant on Chinese nouveau riche flooding in to see castles and highland cows, buying tartan and whisky during the Edinburgh Festival. Or the rich and famous from around the world using wild, unforested Scotland and manicured golf courses for their short-term pleasure. That's a very limited and wasted future.

This may be perceived as an overly depressed view, but we have a strong belief that without carving out a new, special role in the world that will be our long-term fate: a decline into greater poverty, post oil and whisky, in the UK or out of the UK, in Europe or out of Europe.

Final thoughts

One of the authors once heard a wise old engineer talking about the task of reviewing other peoples' designs. He said, "Most engineers are spring-loaded in the critique position. You should find something good, and something to improve." Please read our story in that spirit. We've painted a vision, not a linear plan – impressionist art that leaves room for imagination, not an old master with every detail precisely set out. Is there a part you would like to play in the story, or another scene you'd like to write?

Covid-19 has shaken the world order. Climate change challenges our way of life. Britain, for good or ill, is leaving Europe, Scotland in tow. The old industrial order, including oil, is on its way out, and we are yet to understand our role in the fourth industrial revolution.

So, what is the new world that is relevant for Scotland?

- oil is a thing of the past
- wood is the new material; steel and concrete have had their day
- wind, wave, tides, and sun are the new energy sources
- marine is a new frontier for food and technology
- the Arctic sea ice will inevitably melt, even if climate change is successfully halted
- medical security post Covid-19 is at least as important as energy and military security, maybe more so
- technology, robots and AI will replace humans, even in service and care jobs

- large countries are not needed to create large markets

- Keynesian policies return, after four decades of neoliberalism and austerity

Can Scotland thrive in this new world? Can it turn itself around? Our answer is "absolutely, yes!" Scotland can harness these changes to create a thriving society for all of its people – healthy, wealthy and wise by 2070.

"The best way to predict your future is to create it" – Abraham Lincoln

References for Chapter 8

[1] BiGGAR Economics. *Scotland's Natural Economy: Sustainable Growth Potential* A report to SRUC, July 2020

[2] This phrase came up in conversation with a leading Scottish economist. It seems to originate in a seminar discussion paper by Harvard academics Hausman and Rodrik, *Doomed to choose: industrial policy as predicament*, Kennedy School of Government, 2006

[3] https://www.irishtimes.com/life-and-style/people/tk-whitaker-obituary-1.2930820

[4] http://whitakerinstitute.ie/tk-whitaker-legacy/

[5] Irish Government, *Programme for Economic Expansion*, Stationery Office Dublin, November 1958 https://ptfs-oireachtas.s3.amazonaws.com/DriveH/AWData/Library3/Library2/DL006590.pdf

[6] Mariana Mazzucato, *The Entrepreneurial State*, Penguin, 2015

[7] Kate Raworth, *Doughnut Economics: Seven Ways to Think Like a 21st-Century Economist*, Random House, 2018

[8] Scotland's Inward Investment Plan October- Shaping Scotland's economy 2020.

Acknowledgements

We would like to acknowledge all the people who have helped us during this project. Many have freely offered advice, criticism, help and encouragement. We tried to mention them all here. We are very sorry if we missed anyone.

David Balfour, Hew Balfour, Robert Balfour, Lewis Bowick, Glen Bramley, John Cant, Craig Dalzell, Topher Dawson, Cameron Dobbie, Eric Dobbie, Anna Frame, Russell Gunson, Ellie Harrison, Gerry Hassan, Steve and Donna Heddle, Stephen Ingledew, Jane Johnson, Graeme Jones, Dr Douglas Kennedy, Graham Leicester, Sheena MacDonald, Robin McAlpine, Stuart McIntyre, Gordon McIntyre-Kemp, Mary Margaret McKenzie, Bruce McNaughton, Donald McPhillimy, Jim Mather, Mandy Meikle, Luke Moffat, Jemma Neville, Mike Perks, Lesley Riddoch, Craig Ritchie, Graeme Roy, Gavin Sillitto, Andrew Somerville, Michael Steel, Andrew Wilson,

Rona Sillitto, for her support and her insightful perspectives throughout the project.

Jane Spurr of College Publications for taking the book on and for her support and help in the publishing process; Laraine Welch for turning our hotchpotch of ideas and suggestions into the excellent final cover design; and the graphics professionals, Jasper and Henry Affonso, who created the images throughout the book.

The Edinburgh University student and graduate team who helped us finish the book editorially and launch the website and social media: Francesca Vavotici, Sarah McCallum, and Cameron Somers. Denise Moodaley for her administrative support.

Members of the Edinburgh U3A Climate Change and Advanced Creative Writing groups, and of the Reforesting Scotland Facebook Group.

Halldór Jóhannsson of The Arctic Portal for his insight and permission to use the map in Chapter 2. Thanks also to the organisations IPPR Scotland, Scottish Financial Enterprise, Business for Scotland, Greenbrook Healthcare, and Fintech Scotland.

Key References

Armstrong, Poulsom, Connolly and Peace. *A survey of cattle-grazed woodlands in Britain,* final report, Forest Research, October 2003

Baker, Epstein and Montecino. *The UK's Finance Curse? Costs and Processes.* Sheffield Political Economy Research Institute, 2019

Bastin JF, Finegold Y, Garcia C, Mollicone D, Rezende M, Routh D, Zohner CM, Crowther TW. *The global tree restoration potential.* Science, 5 July 2019

Berners-Lee, Mike, *There's No Planet B*, Cambridge University Press, Cambridge, 2019

BP *Statistical Review of World Energy* 2019

Brack, Duncan and King, Richard. *Net Zero and beyond – what role for Bioenergy with Carbon Capture and Storage?* Chatham House, Jan 2020

Brown, Gordon. *My Scotland, Our Britain*, Simon & Schuster, 2014

Committee on Climate Change. *Reducing emissions in Scotland, 2019 Progress Report to Parliament. Committee on Climate Change* Dec. 2019

Common Weal. *Back to life: visions of alternative futures for Scotland's grouse moors.* Common Weal policy paper, December 2018

Chalmers and Westbrook. *The economic contribution of the forestry sector in Scotland.* CJC Consulting September 2015

Dalzell, Craig. *Good houses for all: how Scotland can build unlimited homes - without subsidy.* Common Weal Policy Paper, May 2020

DNV GL. *Sustainable Blue Economy in the Norwegian Arctic.* Written for the Centre for the Ocean and the Arctic, June 2019.

Dow, Amy - Knoydart ranger. Quoted in John Muir Trust Journal 67 – Autumn 2019

Fern. *Six problems with BECCS.* Fern office, September 2018

Finnish Prime Minister Office. *Action Plan for the Update of the Arctic Strategy.* March 2017,

Forestry Commission. *The UK Forestry Standard: The governments' approach to sustainable forestry.* 2017

Fraser of Allander Institute. *Scotland in 2050- Realising our Global Potential.* University of Strathclyde, March 2019

Hawken, Paul. *Drawdown: The Most Comprehensive Plan Ever Proposed to Reverse Global Warming,* Penguin Books 22 Feb 2018

Harrison, Ellie. *The Glasgow Effect.* Luath, 2019

International Energy Agency – *Sustainable Recovery – world energy outlook special report* – June 2020

IPPR Commission on Economic Justice. *Our Common Wealth, A Citizen's Wealth Fund for the UK,* April 2018

Institute for Public Policy Research, *Transport Investment In The Northern Powerhouse* 2019 update, IPPR North, August 2019

Jozepa, Ilze. *EU State Aid rules and WTO Subsidies Agreement.* House of Commons Library Briefing Paper Number 06775, 12 June 2019

Khorrami, Nima. *Sweden's Arctic Strategy - An Overview.* The Arctic Institute, April 2019.

Knight, J. *A Forest for the Future.* Reforesting Scotland, July 2019

McAlpine R, Dalzell C, and Venables E (Editors). *The Common Home Plan – a green new deal for Scotland.* Common Weal, November 2019

McIntyre-Kemp. G. *Scotland the Brief,* Business for Scotland, January 2020

Main, Lever & Crook. *Central Scotland Airport Study.* David Hume Institute, 2003

Maxwell, Stephen. *Arguing for Independence – Evidence, Risk and Wicked Issues.* Luath, 2012/2013 p.179

Mazzucato M, *The Entrepreneurial State, debunking public versus private sector myths.* Anthem 2013, Penguin Random House UK 2018

Melia, Haines and Hawkins. *Future of the Sea: Implications from Opening Arctic Sea Routes.* UK Government Publication. July 2017

Helliwell, J., Layard, R., & Sachs, J. (2019). *World Happiness Report 2019,* New York: Sustainable Development Solutions Network.

Oil and Gas UK. *Workforce-Report.* OGUK, 2019

Raworth, Kate. *Doughnut Economics: Seven Ways to Think Like a 21st-Century Economist.* Random House, 2018

Reforesting Scotland. *The Impact and Management of Deer in Scotland.* Reforesting Scotland, November 2013

Riddoch, Lesley and Bort, Eberhard. *McSmorgasbord.* Luath Press, 2017

Royal Swedish Academy of Agriculture & Forestry. *Forests and Forestry in Sweden,* August 2015

Scottish Sustainable Growth Commission. Scotland – *The New Case for Optimism - A strategy for inter-generational economic renaissance*. The Sustainable Growth Commission, May 2018

Scott, James. *Minority report to a report by the Game and Heather Burning (Scotland) committee*, 1921

Scottish Forest and Timber Technologies, *Roots for Future Growth* (2011), p. 31

Scottish Financial Enterprise. *Scotland's Financial Services Expertise*. SFE, October 2018

Scottish Government. *Government Expenditure & Revenue Scotland 2017-18*. Scottish Government, 2018

Scottish Government. *Infrastructure Investment Plan 2015 - Progress Report for 2019-20*. Scottish Government, April 2020

Scottish Government. *Scotland's Arctic Policy Framework*. September 2019.

Smil, Vaclav. *Energy in Nature and Society: General Energetics of Complex Systems*. The MIT Press, Cambridge, 2008

Tingay, Ruth, and Wightman, Andy. *The Case for Reforming Scotland's Driven Grouse Moors*. Revive Coalition, Edinburgh, 2018

UK Infrastructure and Projects Authority, *Analysis of the National Infrastructure and Construction Pipeline*. I&PA, November 2018

UN *Global Sustainable Development report* 2019

Wightman, Andy. Essay in *'Scotland the Brave?'* Ed. Hassan, Luath Press, July 2019

Meet the Authors

Ian Godden was born in Edinburgh to an Irish father and Scottish mother. He attained a BSc in Chemical Engineering from Edinburgh University, a Diploma in Accountancy and Finance (CDipAF) and an MBA, Stanford Graduate School of Business. He is a Fellow of the Royal Aeronautical Society (FRAeS).

He joined BP as an engineer and project manager in the early development of Magnus and the Sullom Voe oil terminal and conducted tours of duty in the Middle East. He became a Partner with Booz Allen in Houston, New York and London and a Senior Partner of Roland Berger in Munich, advising Oil and Gas, Chemical and Aerospace & Defence corporations on strategy and the UK, Dutch and South African Governments on industrial policy. He became Chairman of the Trade Association for Aerospace, Defence and Security (ADS) and of Farnborough Airshow. He served as a member of the UK Government's National Defence Industrial Council (NDIC).

In entrepreneurial terms, he co-founded two successful UK businesses- a strategy consulting business, sold to a German company, and a UK medical start-up, Greenbrook Healthcare. He was appointed as Chairman to turnaround an AIM listed software and consulting company, KBC, before it was sold to a Japanese company.

Ian is currently working in the Middle East, advising Governments on Oil and Gas and Defence. He also chairs Bristow Aviation Holdings (UK) that runs the UK's search and rescue helicopter services.

He co-authored a successful business book, Managing Without Management.

He is married with two children and two grandchildren.

Hillary Sillitto was born, brought up and educated in Scotland, gained a BSc(hons) in Physics from St Andrews, and later earned an MSc in Applied Optics at Imperial College. He had a successful engineering career with Ferranti and Thales, with eight successful patent applications. Appointments included Chief Engineer for Thales Optronics, Head of the UK MOD's Integration Authority (on secondment from industry), and Systems Engineering Director for

Thales UK. He is a Chartered Engineer and a Fellow of the Institute of Physics. He is also an internationally recognised expert in Systems Engineering and Systems Science, and one of approximately fifty current Fellows of the International Council on Systems Engineering. He has held visiting professorships at the universities of Bristol and Strathclyde. His book 'Architecting Systems – concepts, principles and practice' was published in 2014, leading to further training and consultancy work, including instructing at a delightful annual Systems Engineering Summer School in Sweden. He is married with two grown up children, both of whom are now, to their parents' delight, living and working back in Scotland. He has always been keen on outdoor activities, 'compleating' the Munros in the mid-80s. Now 'retired' and a grandfather, when time allows he still enjoys exploring wild places in Scotland and further afield, skiing, sailing, photography, birdwatching, and playing the whistle.

Dorothy Godden was born and brought up in India in 1952, at the tail end of the British Empire. Her parents were from Edinburgh, both Scottish Missionaries. Her mother trained as a nurse and midwife and worked as one of the first Health Visitors in the NHS and her father trained as a mathematician and minister. She attended school in Darjeeling and in Dacca.

She returned to Edinburgh with her family in 1965 at the age of 13 and trained as a nurse in the Royal Infirmary, Edinburgh, specializing as a coronary care nurse. After marrying Ian Godden, she practiced nursing in London, Houston and the Bay Area, California. Since returning to the UK in the mid-1980s, she has raised a family and renovated a number of properties in London and Scotland, including historic buildings and gardens in Aviemore and Edinburgh. She has lived in Abu Dhabi for the last six years supporting Ian's business interests. In her spare time, she is a keen gardener and a student of British and Scottish History.

Despite only having lived 10 years in Scotland, she has a passion for Scotland's wellbeing and success. Her daughter moved with their family to Edinburgh from London and her son lives and works in the technology world of Old Street, London. She looks forward to returning from Abu Dhabi to Edinburgh and spending more time with her two grandchildren.